JOHN 17
THE HEART OF GOD

JOHN 17
THE HEART OF GOD

With a Letter
of Introduction
by
Pope Francis

Edited and with a Preface
by
Joseph Tosini

Published by New City Press
202 Comforter Blvd.,
Hyde Park, NY 12538
www.newcitypress.com

Cover design by Peter Petrov
Book design and layout by Miguel Tejerina

JOHN 17, The Heart of God (paperback)

Library of Congress Control Number: 2018943200

ISBN: 978-1-56548-642-3 (paperback)
ISBN: 978-1-56548-651-5 (e-book)

Printed in the United States of America

Contents

Introduction

Vatican, October 2, 2017

Dear beloved brothers and sisters in Christ, May grace and peace be yours in abundance!

I rejoice to hear that on October 24 you are gathering together again to worship our one and only Savior and Lord Jesus Christ and to strengthen one another in the path of unity and reconciliation that you have undertaken.

During your visit, here in Rome, I was blessed to listen to you tell of the encouraging developments in your journey, to celebrate Pentecost together, and to observe the degree of brotherly friendship that has come to exist among you.

My prayer is that the testimony of your lives may draw many others to Christ and that your experience of fellowship may inspire an ever-increasing number of Evangelicals, Pentecostals, and Catholics to rediscover one another, coming together in a mutually redemptive walk of reconciliation. Our desire is to continue to practice and promote an ecumenism based on the unity of the Spirit. This will increasingly bring all of us to free ourselves from the reservations and prejudices that until now have prevented us from walking together, as has always been the will of the Lord.

May Jesus' prayer, which I know is honored among you, be our guiding star... Against every form of intolerance and sectarianism, may it encourage us to walk together, with mutual love, so that our witness to the world may become more and more credible, visible, and effective. My beloved sisters and brothers, we all need the Lord's blessing. For my part, I bless you and I ask for your blessing upon me as I embrace you with all my heart. Please do not forget, all of you who are taking part in this Meeting for Reconciliation, to pray for me.

May the Lord bless you all. Brotherly greetings in Christ,

Franciscus

Preface

Division is the culture of today. Racial, religious, gender, political, and generational differences can no longer be discussed with civility and respect. Ridicule and disdain are the platforms for debating opposing opinions, and too often hatred resulting in violence is the preferred method of finding a solution. Yet in this book you will find a diverse group of Christian leaders declaring that the world is on an ever-faster journey toward unity. And we are not just declaring it; we are deeply convinced that this is the future.

To hold such a solid conviction when the world increasingly embraces a message of liberation from institutions with archaic ideologies and practices probably seems naïve to some readers. To believe it as Christians when there are thirty-four thousand denominations (and growing) in the world, each professing a different understanding of what it means to be the Body of Christ, seems absurd. In the mind of many, unity is not something to strive for but an evil to avoid. The 2017 New Year's Eve celebration in Times Square climaxed with John Lennon's song "Imagine." Lennon sings of a new order where countries and religions are gone, implying that without them, greed, hunger, and war would vanish and be replaced by true brotherhood. *Unity* would be the result; we could, as the song concludes, "live as one." As nice a sentiment as this may be, this is not the unity that this book and its contributors have in mind.

The contributors to this book, starting with the author of the Introduction, have their eyes wide open and are aware that there are no easy solutions to the divisions growing among us and around us. We take with great seriousness the January 1, 2018, "red alert" message of the Secretary General of the United Nations, António Guterres. "When I took office one year ago, I appealed for 2017 to be a year for peace," he said. "Unfortunately—in fundamental ways, the world has gone in reverse. . . . I urge leaders everywhere to make this New Year's resolution: Narrow the gaps. Bridge the divides. Rebuild trust by bringing people together around common goals. Unity is the path. Our future depends on it."[1] Destroying institutions is not the answer, he cries, but instead contributes to our demise.

Division is spreading and unity is direly needed. As Guterres clearly states, it is an imperative for the future. Why are the contributors to this book so convinced that things will turn out for the better, that unity is possible? The answer lies in the seventeenth chapter of John's Gospel. It is known as the testament and final prayer of Jesus. In it he prays to the Father that his disciples will be one. The goal of this book is to help crystallize Jesus' prayer for unity. It is the only solution for the Church's diminishing effect in a world that is relationally broken at its core. The basis of Jesus' message is found in his actions that follow this prayer, which are expressions of his love. Those who are part of this book are part of a much larger movement of the Spirit that desires to live out John chapter 17. In fact, that is the name we have given ourselves: the John 17 Movement.

I am certain most would agree that love is not only the answer but also the most powerful force in all creation. Scripture states clearly, "God is love" (1 John 4:8). Love is the fuel and foundation of true generosity, justice, mercy, forgiveness, genuine faith, and hope. Epistemologically it is the starting and finishing point of all knowing. The most notable civil rights leader, Rev. Dr. Martin Luther King, Jr., famously stated, "I am convinced that love is the most durable power in the world. It is not an expression of impractical idealism; but of practical realism. Far from being the pious

---

1. "New Year's Message from UN Secretary-General António Guterres: An Alert for the World" December 31, 2017. https://unama. unmissions.org/new-year%E2%80%99s-message-un-secretary-general-ant%C3%B3nio-guterres-alert-world.

injunction of a Utopian dreamer, love is an absolute necessity for the survival of our civilization."[2]

A close study of John chapter 17, and the entire New Testament, reveals that the outcome of love is unity. It turns out to be the necessary ingredient for the Church to be "the light of the world," the "salt of the earth," and "the city on a hill" as Jesus intended.

At this point, the important question is, what does this unity we are speaking about look like? Is it highly subjective, requiring unique insight or superior intelligence? Does it demand certain political allegiances? Is it confined within the boundaries of ethnic identities? Is it limited to those who agree on all points of denominational and religious dogmas?

In Luke's Gospel an expert in the law asks Jesus a similarly important question: "What must I do to inherit eternal life?" Jesus answered with a question of his own, "What is written in the law? What do you read there?" The expert in the law recited, "You shall love the lord your God with all your heart, and with all your soul, and with all your strength, and with all your mind; and your neighbor as yourself." Jesus' reply is key to understanding God's will for all of us. "You have given the right answer; do this, and you will live" (Luke 10:25-28; cf. Deuteronomy 6:5).

The lawyer's response is (and I'm paraphrasing here), "Hold on a minute, who is my neighbor?" Jesus replies, "I'm glad you asked." He then tells the now-famous Good Samaritan story of the Jewish man who, while traveling on a deserted road, was robbed, beaten, and left to die. Two religious people who were also Jewish passed by without stopping to give assistance. Then a Samaritan, considered a second-class person, came by and acted with compassion, not considering the sociological division of the culture. He

---

2. Martin Luther King, Jr., "Advice for Living," November 1957, in *The Papers of Martin Luther King, Jr. Volume IV: Symbol of the Movement, January 1957-December 1958*, eds. Clayborne Carson, Susan Carson, Adrienne Clay, Virginia Shadron, and Kieran Taylor (Berkeley: University of California Press, 2000), 306.

physically assisted the wounded man, then took him to a safe place and paid for his care. Jesus then asked the lawyer, "Which of these three, do you think, was a neighbor to the man who fell into the hands of robbers?" The expert in the law replied, "The one who showed him mercy." The end of this exchange is key to the vision of this book and how its contributors understand John chapter 17. Jesus said, "Go and do likewise" (see Luke 10:29-37).

The pursuit of that expression of love will produce the unity for which Jesus prayed. This kind of unity will result in the satisfaction and rest the human heart is longing for. Augustine of Hippo said it best, "You have made us and drawn us to yourself, and our heart is unquiet until it rests in you."[3] In Rabbi Hayim Halevy Donin's book *To Pray as a Jew*, he argues, "technology may have advanced, cultures may have changed, but human nature and the human condition have remained constant."[4] King Solomon, with the gift of wisdom God gave him, said, "He has also set eternity in the human heart" (Ecclesiastes 3:11, NIV). What is that heavenly download all about? Relationship. The deepest joy and sorrow come from our relationships, not our things or accomplishments. There are myriads of examples to prove it, but rather than give some, I would like you to take a moment and ask yourself these questions: *When was the happiest, most satisfying time in my life? When was the saddest?* I suspect both will involve relationships.

The last night of Jesus' life on earth has one clear overriding theme: God's love for us and his desire that we love one another *as* he loves us. I like to place two bookends on that last Passover meal: the washing of the disciples' feet and Jesus' prayer prior to exiting for Gethsemane.

---

3. Saint Augustine, *The Confessions*, trans. Maria Boulding, OSB, ed. John E. Rotelle, OSA (Hyde Park: New City Press, 2001), 14.
4. Rabbi Hayim Halevy Donin, *To Pray As A Jew: A Guide To The Prayer Book And The Synagogue Service* (New York: Basic Books, 1991), 6.

In the washing of the feet Jesus clothes himself with the apron of a servant. He kneels at the feet of his disciples and he washes their feet. When finished, he takes off the apron, puts his robe back on, takes his seat, and says, "Do you know what I have done to you? You call me Teacher and Lord—and you are right, for that is what I am" (John 13:12-13). He then explains that the example he gave them is to be followed by each of them. They will be blessed by doing, not just knowing. A key point we in John 17 believe is that Jesus taught us relationship begins at the feet, not the head. It's easy to exchange ideas, theories, methodologies, etc. That's more of a head-to-head encounter. Beginning at the feet, however, is where vulnerability and friendships are formed.

The other bookend is Jesus' prayer. It is the longest prayer we hear Jesus pray in the Gospels. The only other major prayer was in response to the disciples' request about how they should pray. It could be said that what we call the "Lord's Prayer" is more correctly the disciples' prayer. This prayer in John chapter 17, however, is without question the Lord's prayer. The clear takeaway from this intense prayer to the Father is the Lord's desire that the unity that exists in the Trinity be made available to all of us. There is no way of fully comprehending that, at least on this side of eternity. Nevertheless, it is clear that God has redeemed us for that purpose. It is also clear that our unity is the greatest evidence we can show to those outside of the Christian faith that Jesus is who he said he is: the true Savior and Lord of all.

Jesus told his disciples they were his friends. He went on to give us two key aspects of friendship. One, that he did not withhold from them what the Father had told him. He shared it all (cf. John 15:15). Two, that friendship is costly. In John 15:12 Jesus gave his disciples a new command, "love one another as I have loved you." He then defined that love command more clearly: "to lay down one's life for one's friends" (John 15:13). That kind of love is the evidence of our friendship with Jesus and with each other.

One of my dearest friends, Pastor Giovanni Traettino, had the privilege of meeting Cardinal Jorge Bergoglio a number of years ago in Argentina. Their relationship grew over the years and when Cardinal Bergoglio became Pope Francis, like all genuine friendships, it continued. Since Giovanni lived in Italy, the geographical distance between them was shortened with this new development. I will share more of this story later in the book. My point is, friends have a natural desire to share with their friends. This is how I had the honor of meeting Pope Francis some years ago. Since then, a number of us in the John 17 Movement have had the privilege to meet with the pope. The way this happened is very much the point we are trying to convey in this book. The will of God is best expressed in friendship.

The testimonies you will read or listen to in these chapters are stories of men and women from different parts of the Lord's Church: Anglican, Catholic, Charismatic, Evangelical, Orthodox, Pentecostal, etc. Each have been privileged to meet together in friendship and brotherhood with Pope Francis. Their encounters have healed, inspired, and helped form a spirituality that has come to be known as the John 17 Movement. As Pope Francis has said so profoundly, "Let's have a gelato; take a walk. When we do, unity has begun."

Joseph Tosini
Phoenix, Arizona

Finding My Identity

Joseph Tosini

"Remember, Giuseppe, you are American of Italian descent." Those were always strange words to me, yet to my grandmother they were of the utmost importance. I spent my formative years under the influence of my paternal grandparents, who both came to America from Italy. Their love and appreciation for being in America was a daily sermon starting and ending with "God bless America" in broken English.

It took me many years to understand how dramatic a change they had made. In their hearts and minds they had embraced a new identity. They were no longer Italians; they were now Americans, always adding "of Italian descent." I often think of the implications of that transition—the separation from what was natural and secure, like family, surroundings, language, and culture—and replacing all of that with always feeling a bit out of place. Their experience serves as a good analogy for what happened to me when Jesus, by his grace, revealed himself to me and I received him as my Lord and Savior. Though I did not realize it at that moment, my identity had been changed.

As a young adult in the late 1960s I landed in what is known as ground zero of the free speech movement: Berkeley, California. During that time there was a deep unrest within the hearts of my generation seeking a new path. Songs often tell the story of the times. "There's a whole generation with a new explanation," was part of Scott McKenzie's song

"San Francisco." The new explanation, in a word, was love. Many voices called for people to embrace it. "Come on people now, smile on your brother, everybody get together, try and love one another right now," the Youngbloods implored. "All you need is love," the Beatles proclaimed. Love, at least a minimal understanding of it, was the core message of the day.

That desire to love drew me instead to a place of despair. I discovered I did not have the capacity to love unselfishly, nor did anyone around me. My story wasn't unique or unusual during those days. I believe today, decades later, we are feeling the effects of a generation looking for a new path. But in that place of hopelessness, Jesus changed my life forever. A seed was placed in my heart that continues to blossom today.

In 1974 I had just taken the position of associate pastor at a small church in a Midwest college town. One of my responsibilities was to register our campus ministry with the university. The day I went to campus to get the application something quite dramatic happened.

It was the beginning of the school year and there were a number of groups sitting at tables recruiting students to their particular organizations. As I walked past the many tables I noticed a number of different Christian organizations, seven, to be exact.

I stopped walking and just looked at those seven different groups. It was as if I was paralyzed, just staring, when I heard a voice, only audible to me. "Think back to a time not many years ago when I had no place of significance in your life. What would be the first thought that would come to your mind on seeing these seven tables?" Without hesitation I found myself saying in a soft voice, "seven different Jesuses."

We all have seminal moments that change our direction or start paradigm shifts in our thinking: this was one of mine. All of my theological training on the distinctive features of my particular denomination suddenly and without warning collided with this one thought: "Jesus isn't a polygamist." The result of that encounter transformed my understanding of the Church. It was a transition of seeing the Church through God's lens rather than my own. Our uniqueness isn't in what separates Christians into different silos, labeled Protestant, Catholic, or Orthodox. Our uniqueness is what unites us. Jesus only has one spouse, and he affectionately named her Church.

This new understanding was like rocket fuel to my young idealistic heart. Over the next four years the church I pastored experienced rapid numerical growth. By 1978 we had also developed a pastoral fellowship and personal friendships with leaders among the different denominations in our area, both Catholics and non-Catholics. There were gatherings attended by Christians of all types, where we prayed, worshiped, and enjoyed fellowshipping together. There was no competition or anxiety, just profound communion.

Unfortunately, things began to change slowly. People in authority opposed this type of interaction. After all, we had different labels that distinguished us from others professing the same faith. We were Catholic, Orthodox, and all sorts of Protestants: Baptist, Lutheran, Presbyterian, Anglican, Methodist, Pentecostal, Evangelical, charismatic, etc. In addition, many of those groups had subsets further distinguishing them from other professing Christians. Many of those in authority said, "We do not want to confuse our people with differing perspectives."

What I discovered at that young age was that the distinctions between the different denominations and non-denominations had become our identity. We were not acting like Christians of Catholic descent or Protestant descent. We were acting as though we were Catholics and Protestants of Christian descent, as though our denomination was more important than our shared identity. Over the next few years my direction, I'm sad to say, shifted from what unites us as Christians to what distinguishes and divides us. I received my identity not from Jesus alone but from my distinguished group, which was by design separated from the others.

One night in 2013, right after Pope Francis was elected, I was awakened a little after 3:00 a.m. I sensed an urge to pray. Entering our living room and turning on a lamp, I began to ask the Lord what I should be praying for. It seemed so strange when the words, "Pray for my servant Francis," came to me. I instantly knew it was the new pope. It was awkward at first since I am not Catholic. Then, as I began to pray, I felt the presence of the Holy Spirit.

During that prayer time I was reminded of the experience I had in 1974, walking on the campus, seeing those seven tables, and hearing God's voice. My wife Mary awakened and came into the living room to ask me what happened. To both our bewilderment, I told her I thought I was going to meet this new pope and to begin praying and working for unity among Christians again.

I was unaware, but would soon discover, that a dear Italian friend of many years had, by God's doing, developed a friendship with Pope Francis prior to his becoming pope. This was quite a surprise. When I was in Italy shortly after that early morning experience I had the opportunity to speak with my friend Giovanni. He told me of his personal journey of becoming committed to reconciliation among believers. I then learned of how he first met Pope Francis. I shared my experience and the call I felt to work for unity among Christians, living out the seventeenth chapter of John's Gospel, Jesus' prayer to the Father. Later, when we were thinking about what to call this movement, Mary said, "Why not just name it what you've been teaching—John 17?"

It was not long after that I felt a prompting to ask Giovanni to come to Phoenix, Arizona, where Mary and I lived part of the year, and share his story. I requested that he ask Pope Francis for a letter of support[5] for the efforts of John 17. When I received word Giovanni could come, and

---

5. Pope Francis's messages to the leaders and members of John 17 are included on pages 165-169 of this book.

the pope would send his blessing, I called the Catholic bishop's office in Phoenix to ask for a meeting.

We met with the bishop of Phoenix, Thomas Olmsted, and the auxiliary bishop, Eduardo Nevares. In the providence of God, Bishop Olmsted had a change in his schedule and was able to join us for all three of our early John 17 gatherings. I must confess that those meetings had a profound impact on me. I found myself examining my journey as a believer, the ups and downs as well as the times of personal disappointment in myself. I had to confront the harshness in my own heart toward those outside my unique tribe of Christians. I asked both the Lord and Bishop Olmsted for forgiveness for my attitudes toward the Catholic Church.

At our first meeting we had a lunch hosted by a pastors' fellowship called Grace Association. We invited other Evangelical pastors to join, and many did. It was at that meeting, sharing a meal together, that a barrier of division was taken away. Picture this setting: two Catholic bishops, a Pentecostal pastor with two Catholic leaders from Italy, and thirty-plus Evangelical pastors from the valley of Phoenix.

I was to introduce our guests from Italy along with the bishops. I had come down with laryngitis, so my voice was extremely hoarse. Giovanni joked on the way over that I sounded like Marlon Brando in *The Godfather*. When I made the introductions, I spontaneously said in that godfather voice, "I came here today from New York and brought some friends from the 'don' in Rome. We are here to make the peace." Of course the room filled with laughter. I then added, looking at the bishops, "If there are any here today that do not want to make the peace, we have to report back to the 'don' in Rome. I want to be clear, I can't protect you."

That was the introduction, and what followed in all the sharing back and forth was, I believe, a clarity and acknowledgement understood by all. We are first and foremost brothers and sisters in Christ Jesus. God has one family. Each of us, as leaders, and those we represent are a part of that one family. Our family is divided and we want to do our part in narrowing those divides. Those three days were the official inauguration of the John 17 Movement. Since that time Mary and I, along with an ever-increasing number of brothers and sisters from various streams of Christianity, have been committed to pursuing the unity Jesus prayed for in John chapter 17.

Like my grandparents found, it's always difficult to adjust our identities. It can be uncomfortable and confusing at first. We can and should celebrate where we have come from, and not dismiss our unique heritages. These heritages have much to contribute alongside all of the other varieties in God's garden. But we must not allow our particular group to be the whole, to be our entire identity. God has made us to be a part of one family, his family. This is to be what distinguishes us as Christians in this world that is searching for true identity. As I heard my precious grandmother say many times, "Remember, Giuseppe, you are American of Italian descent." In the same way I hear Jesus say, "Remember, Giuseppe, your new identity is in me alone."

Unity: God's Plan

Mike Herron

Joseph and Giovanni

I first met Joseph Tosini in 1979 when I was the worship leader at Bible Temple Church in Portland, Oregon, and he was the founding pastor of Christian Fellowship, a non-denominational charismatic church in Columbia, Missouri. We were drawn to each other through our mutual love and respect for the presence of the Lord that accompanied the biblical understanding of worship. My church was an early pioneer in the charismatic expression of the contemporary Christian worship movement and I visited his congregation repeatedly to teach and encourage their worship team.

In 1982 Joseph traveled to Italy and met Giovanni Traettino, an Italian Pentecostal pastor of a fellowship of churches centered in the city of Caserta. Giovanni is the spiritual father of the reconciliation movement between Catholics and Protestants. Joseph offered to return with me in early 1983 to minister at a worship seminar with the approximately thirty churches connected with Giovanni's ministry team. Joseph called me with great excitement and said, "Mike, we're going to have a worship conference in Italy next year!" I told him that would be impossible because I was planting a church in Salem, Oregon, in January and would not be traveling at all that first year. Realizing that I was fully resolved not to go, Joseph asked me to pray and told me he would call back in one hour. Whatever the Lord led me to do, he would abide by that.

21

For fifty-five minutes, I did not pray, as I was sure that God didn't want me to go to Italy. Knowing that Joseph would call exactly on the hour, I eventually got on my knees and began praying, "Lord, I know you don't want me to go to Italy . . ." I was unwisely providing the answer to my own prayer. In those few minutes the thought kept going through my head, "Acts 27 . . . Acts 27." I opened my Bible to Acts 27:1 and read, "When it was decided that we were to sail for Italy . . ." Immediately the phone rang and Joseph asked, "How has the Lord answered your prayer?" Incredulous, I asked him if he had ever noticed this scripture. After reading it he laughed and replied, "Well, I guess we are going to Italy!" That trip turned out to be a major turning point in our lives that reverberates until this day, as well as the beginning of our friendship with Pastor Giovanni Traettino.

Matteo Calisi

The conference on worship was small in numbers but large in impact. Several key pastors and worship leaders in the Italian Evangelical movement were there. Each time I shared with the group of around thirty-five people, I was drawn to a young man that I would later come to know, Matteo Calisi. At the end of the conference Joseph and I asked him to come forward. We prayed over him and shared what God was putting in our hearts. Not knowing that he was the only Catholic attending the conference, we told him that we were given the impression that God was going to use him in a great way in the worship ministry in the Roman Catholic Church throughout the world. In the subsequent years, Matteo has constantly referred to that moment as a word of destiny to him and his ministry. He did go on to become a major figure in the Catholic charismatic movement. He leads the Charismatic Community of Jesus in Bari, Italy, and is involved in several other organizations focused on the unity of the Body of Christ. This was the beginning of our lifetime of friendship and collaboration in the work of Christian unity.

Gatherings in the Holy Spirit

Giovanni and Matteo formed a close friendship and began traveling together as Protestant and Catholic to share the message of Christian unity and reconciliation among believers in all denominations. They invited me to The Gathering in the Holy Spirit at the *Centro Pro Unione* (Center for Unity) in Rome in 1999. It was a conversation among non-denominational Christians and Roman Catholics. There I got to hear and become friends with some of the profound teachers and leaders of the Catholic charismatic movement: Fr. Peter Hocken, Fr. Raniero Cantalamessa, O.F.M. Cap., Charles Whitehead, and Dr. Kevin Ranaghan. I attended the gathering four different times in the span of seven years and gained a new understanding and appreciation of the 2000 years of rich spiritual heritage we have from the Catholic Church.

There is One

I began to see more clearly God's plan of unity from Ephesians 4:4-6: "there is one body" (ecclesiology) made of true believers from all the denominations of Christianity; "and one Spirit" (pneumatology) that regenerates and fills every believer with eternal life and is working to bring about unity in our age. There is "one hope of [our] calling" (eschatology), Christ's return, the resurrection and the new heavens and earth where all Christians will live as one. There is "one Lord" (Christology); "Jesus is Lord" is the condensed creed of the Church age. There is "one faith," one act of trust in Christ that universally connects all believers; and "one baptism" (soteriology), one act of obedience that unites Christians around the world. There is "one God and Father of all, who is above all and through all and in all" (theology).

There is only one family of God and we must accept and love all those whom he has received as his children.

23

Pope Francis

In 2005, Pentecostal pastor Jorge Himitian invited Giovanni to visit his church in Argentina. While there Giovanni met a group of Catholics who asked him to return and speak at a large ecumenical gathering. Unable to attend, Giovanni suggested that they invite the preacher of the papal household, Fr. Raniero Cantalamessa, in his place. Fr. Cantalamessa happily accepted the invitation and, as things turned out, Giovanni's schedule changed and he was able to come as well. Cardinal Jorge Bergoglio, then archbishop of Buenos Aires, was invited to this event and agreed to come but chose to be seated with the public and not in the platform. At the request of the organizers, he came to listen to the Pentecostal preacher Giovanni Traettino and remained very impressed. At the end of the meeting, Cardinal Bergoglio was invited to address the crowd. When he finished his remarks, he kneeled down on his knees and asked the people to pray for him. So, the pastors, Evangelical and Catholic, and the 6,000 people in the stadium did that, with raised hands. The first prayer was by Pastor Carlos Mraida and the second one by Fr. Cantalamessa. It was a special moment. As the prayer ended, Fr. Cantalamessa exclaimed, "May his voice be heard all over the world." Cardinal Bergoglio began an important journey of friendship with Giovanni and other pastors present that day.

Shortly after the cardinal was elected as pope in 2013, Giovanni received a call on his cell phone while driving in his car with his son Luigi. Luigi answered, and a voice said, "This is Pope Francis and I would like to speak with Giovanni Traettino." Luigi, thinking it was a joke replied, "Yeah, and this is Saint Peter." The same exchange was repeated a second time and after a pause Pope Francis said, "My son, this is truly Francis, and I want to speak with my friend Giovanni." Pope Francis went on to invite Giovanni and his wife Franca to visit him many times in the Vatican to share prayer and friendship. There was just one proviso: Franca had to bring her special cake, which is the pope's favorite!

Phoenix

Joseph and I had been planning a gathering for pastors and leaders in the Phoenix area to be held in the spring of 2014. Joseph, a "big idea" person, called me and said, "Why don't we ask Giovanni to get a letter from Pope Francis endorsing a gathering of Catholics and Evangelicals and present it to the bishops of Phoenix, Bishop Tom Olmsted and Auxiliary Bishop Eduardo Nevares, and invite all the Catholic and Protestant leaders in Phoenix to attend?" Some ideas are so grand that they can only have their origin in heaven, and this seemed to be one of them.

We did get a letter from Pope Francis that was delivered personally by Giovanni. We made an appointment with the bishops at the Diocesan Center in downtown Phoenix. Seated around a large conference table, Joseph Tosini, Giovanni Traettino, Matteo Calisi, Pastor Gary Kinnaman, and myself greeted Bishops Olmsted and Nevares. Joseph was our main spokesperson and he slid the letter across the expanse of the table and invited Bishop Olmsted to attend the upcoming meetings, complete with his *Godfather* impersonation. After reading the letter, the bishop smiled and said, "That is funny, really funny!" He went on, "Well, I don't have a letter from Pope Francis, and if he is for this, I will be there."

This was a special moment for the birth of the John 17 Movement both in Phoenix and around the world. The unity gatherings and goodwill expressed in the city among Catholics and Evangelicals are a model for every city, town, and region. "That they may become completely one, so that the world may know that you sent me and have loved them even as you have loved me" (John 17:23). Our unity validates our faith as being genuine and true.

Caserta

In June 2014 I received a phone call from Giovanni inviting my wife Marsha and me to come to his church in Caserta the following month, as Pope Francis would be there for a special visit. The pope wanted to make a public apology on behalf of the Roman Catholic Church for their persecution and intolerance towards the Italian Pentecostals in the 20th century. But he realized that the original date of the meeting, July 26, was the Feast of St. Anne, the mother of Mary and the patron saint of Caserta. Not wanting to offend his own Church members or the city of Caserta, he came and held a Mass on that Saturday that was attended by over two hundred thousand people. He returned on Monday, July 28, to hold the meeting with the Pentecostals.

Pope Francis entered the service walking arm in arm with his friend up to the platform. The pope insisted that no Catholic clergy were to be present except for those Giovanni invited, because the meeting was intended for the Pentecostals. The worship began with a very familiar Spanish song (translated into Italian) written by my friend Juan Salinas, "Bendito Jesús." The pope knew the song, since it had been sung in Argentina, and he lifted his hands in praise and joined us in the singing.

Pope Francis's message was not scripted. He began by saying, "Joseph's brothers went to Egypt thinking they would find some food but found their brother instead. I have come here and found you, my brothers and sisters in Christ." Later he went on to ask forgiveness: "I want you, the Pentecostals, to forgive us, the Catholic Church, for the sin of persecution against you in the past years." There was silence and tears, which eventually turned into a standing ovation and cheers. My thoughts at this moment were, "I can believe in a leader who asks forgiveness for their faults." We were watching a miraculous demonstration of a humble act of reconciliation between brothers and sisters.

After the meeting that was attended by around 450 people, a smaller group of around fifty pastors and leaders were invited to a luncheon and dialogue with the pope. The women of the church prepared the meal and set a special crystal, china, and silver place setting for Francis; the rest of us simply had "church plastic" settings. When the pope saw the difference, he asked for the china to be removed so that he would be treated like the rest of us.

After the meal, we were able to ask him questions. The first was, "What is the most difficult thing you have encountered on your pathway to unity?" His answer was immediate: "Fundamentalists who refuse to dialogue; they retreat into their positions and hurl hateful comments towards others." Then he said, "You do not have to give up your identity to dialogue as we are doing here today." This was a very important thought for me. Christian reconciliation does not mean compromising your beliefs but rather expressing them humbly; dialogue demands reality. The pope's vision of unity did not include everyone rejoining the Catholic Church. He also shared his thoughts that Christian unity starts with friendship, not doctrinal uniformity. When asked by a pastor how to do that, he answered, "First greet one another." (laughter) "Don't try to do high things, get a gelato and take a walk together, then unity begins."

The simplicity of his vision of unity was refreshing and doable. He went on to say that theologians are necessary but the point at which they would be likely to agree on all doctrines is the day after the Lord returns. "We do not have time to wait for that day; reconciliation begins at the feet, not the head." He stressed that we must make every effort to love each other, because this is the prayer of Jesus in John chapter 17.

Rome

In both 2016 and 2017 we had the privilege of leading two different groups of around fifty people to Rome to spend over two hours each time in an informal dialogue with Pope Francis. The groups consisted of pastors and their spouses, individuals, and Catholic leaders. We met on both occasions in the afternoon in a smaller reception hall in the Vatican. The pope's warmth and informality set a friendly tone for the meeting.

The first question on the minds of our Evangelical/Pentecostal/Protestant family is, "Is Jesus the only Lord and Savior for mankind?" Pope Francis's answer is always swift and affirmative: "There is no other Savior and Lord but Jesus Christ. He is the only way to God." One of the simplest questions presented to him was, "What do we teach our children?" In part of his answer he said, "Teach them to worship, for worship is prayer without self-interest." This statement had much meaning for me because worship has been a big part of my lifelong ministry. Another thing that impressed me was the pope's love of scripture and his ability to reference it when answering questions. He seems to embody the attitude of Jesus in his love for all believers in Christ.

Around the World

The vision for Christian unity based on friendship continues to grow beyond Phoenix, Arizona, and Caserta and Bari, Italy. In my own city of Houston, Texas, Cardinal Daniel DiNardo has hosted two initiatives gathering pastors and priests together in our city. I attended a meeting in Portland, Oregon, hosted by Imago Dei Church where Peter Smith, the auxiliary bishop of Portland, Josh Butler, the associate pastor of Imago Dei, Joseph Tosini, and myself explained the vision of relational reconciliation. We have also had great progress in northern New York with Pastor Don Curry leading reconciliation efforts with Catholic bishop Terry LaValley and local priests and pastors. I attended the first *Somos Um* (We Are One) conference in Rio de Janeiro, Brazil, in July 2017 with Catholic and Protestant leaders. There, I had the privilege of leading the prayer of reconciliation and unity over Cardinal Orani João Tempesta and the mayor of the city, Marcelo Crivella (who is also a Pentecostal bishop), and his wife Sylvia. The winds of reconciliation are beginning to blow throughout the earth.

Don't stop him!

"John said to [Jesus], 'Teacher, we saw someone casting out demons in your name, and we tried to stop him, because he was not following us.' But Jesus said, 'Do not stop him. . . . Whoever is not against us is for us.'" (Mark 9:38-40).

So much effort has been made within Christianity to oppose other Christians because they are not "following us." We have also been misled to believe that indifference is acceptable with God when we are grudgingly not *against* certain brothers and sisters but not *for* them. We have mistakenly thought that only those who are explicitly *for* us are the ones we are obligated to love and receive in fellowship. But Christ expands our understanding of the scope of his family: "Whoever gives you a cup of water to drink because you bear the name of Christ will by no means lose the reward" (Mark 9:41). The John 17 Movement seeks to build relational unity in the Body of Christ through the small cups of water of love and friendship. If Jesus instructs us not to stop others because they are not in our group, we should not attempt to stop *him* in his great plan of Christian unity.

Charity in All Things

Don Curry

My personal journey toward Christian unity began long before I heard about the John 17 Movement. It began abruptly and unexpectedly in the wee hours of the morning in 1979 while I was a third-year mechanical engineering student at Rochester Institute of Technology (RIT).

Several months earlier, I had had an encounter with Christ that dramatically affected me and helped me understand that Jesus was not only a historical figure who had died for a cause, but was very much alive and wanted a relationship with me. Although raised Roman Catholic, I was biblically illiterate, so when I began to read scripture for the very first time, the words leapt off the page and it seemed like I was having a personal conversation with the author of the Bible.

Not long after this encounter, one evening I finished studying and knelt beside my bed to pray. I began to desperately cry out to God for mercy. The more scripture I read, the more it became clear how much I needed his help, and yet I had no idea what to do or how to change my life. After a time of prayer, not realizing what was happening, I began to see a vision for what seemed like minutes but turned out to be over an hour.

In brief, here is the vision, which not only set the course for my life, but also was a significant factor in what attracted me to the John 17 Movement years later. In the vision, I was viewing the continental United States from above, and then gradually the scene shifted to be over the northeastern United States, until finally the map in front of me kept coming closer and closer until all I could see was the top half of New York State, extending up to the Canadian border. As this portion of New York emerged, out from the center of the map a fire started, like the opening scene from the old *Bonanza* television series, and it consumed the entire landscape. Suddenly, I was on the ground, visiting local churches all over this region of the state. In each local church a message of "unity and revival" was trumpeted. Each time it was proclaimed, there were people who wholeheartedly received the message, and equally as many who vehemently rejected and opposed it. Nonetheless, before long this message gained traction; churches from different denominations and independent congregations began to dialogue, meet together, and walk in visible unity. However, those who had rejected the message of unity aggressively protested and rallied to stop what was happening, until legal force and lethal violence were used to block what the Holy Spirit was doing in the churches.

After this troubling and lengthy spiritually charged experience, I was breathless and had no idea what had happened to me. Having no frame of reference through which to understand it, I called a friend who was a leader in his local church and asked him to help me. He instructed me to turn to the book of Acts and read chapter 2. As a relatively new Christ follower, not only did I not understand what he was telling me, but I also didn't understand how this scripture reference applied to what had just happened, even though it said in verse 17, "your young men shall see visions." I apologized for waking him up, politely said "Thank you," and went to bed.

But I began to study that text and many others from that time on, and to voraciously read Church history and the biographies of legendary Christian leaders who helped change the world. As I gained knowledge of how the Holy Spirit had moved in scripture, as well as in Church history, the vision I saw provided guiderails for the career decisions that I needed to make upon graduation from RIT.

Though I received several job offers, I accepted an engineering position with General Motors (GM) in Massena, New York, because it was in the footprint of the vision I had seen two years prior. After nine wonderful years working for GM, I left industry behind to become the principal of a private Christian school, operated by New Testament Church (NTC), the non-denominational church my wife Mary and I attended in Massena. This decision was the first of many that eventually led me to become the lead pastor of NTC in 1994.

Three years after becoming the team leader of NTC, I had another experience that would move me in the direction of relational reconciliation, the core message of John 17. One night I was awakened around 3:00 a.m., and clearly heard in my mind that I needed to "contact and ask forgiveness from the pastors in Massena." My immediate reaction was, "That's crazy, I'm tired and have never done anything offensive to any of these pastors." Though I repeatedly tried to dismiss the thought and return to sleep, it was impossible because I was so deeply troubled by what I had heard. When morning finally arrived, I contacted a number of local churches and asked to speak with their pastors. In each case, I asked the pastor if they would meet with me, along with several other pastors from the community.

Within a week, five local church pastors met in the basement of an Episcopal church. I began the conversation by saying, "I have asked you here to ask for your forgiveness. Over the years New Testament Church has grown, in some cases at your expense, and I wanted to ask your forgiveness. Did you ever receive a phone call when people left your church and began attending NTC? Did anyone from NTC ever reach out to you to dialogue?" They all affirmed that no one had ever contacted them, so I reiterated how sorry I was and asked for their forgiveness again. With silence hanging in the room, I described what had happened to me several nights earlier, when I awakened and knew I needed to ask them for forgiveness.

An additional impression I received that pivotal night was that if we as pastors prayed together for an increase of the Holy Spirit's activity in our region, our churches would all go higher in God's purpose, like boats affected by the tide when it rises, and together we would have a greater influence and impact in our community. From that first meeting, God moved in our hearts, and as a group of pastors we became good friends and began to pray together regularly. Soon other local pastors joined us, and we prayed together every week for five years and every other week for five more! After that decade of praying together, another pastor assumed the responsibility of getting us together to pray, and we continued for several more years.

Since that first meeting, we have also gone away on prayer retreats, shared many breakfasts, conducted community prayer walks with our churches, held fundraisers for local food pantries, supplied more than 8,400 homes in Massena with the Jesus video, had many joint worship and prayer services, and even started a community summer event called "LOVE Massena" in a troubled neighborhood, which resulted from a conversation with the mayor. This one event has become an annual community tradition. Because of our positive influence in the community, our churches were invited by the mayor to participate in difficult conversations with New York state, county, and local agencies regarding suicide and substance abuse, as well as how to better support and care for the veterans in our community.

To this day, there is a lasting friendship across denominational lines in Massena among Roman Catholics, Congregationalists, Baptists, Assemblies of God, Episcopalians, Advent Christians, and non-denominational churches, as well as with community leaders.

In February of 2015, I was introduced to the John 17 Movement by my longtime friend Mike Herron of Houston, Texas, and his good friend Matteo Calisi from Bari, Italy. While Mike and Matteo were in Massena, we were able to meet with the local Roman Catholic bishop and several priests in the diocese as well as a number of Evangelical, Pentecostal, and Charismatic pastors. Shortly after these meetings Mike was invited to attend a gathering in Caserta, Italy, where Pope Francis would visit Pastor Giovanni Traettino's Pentecostal church. For us it was astounding to think a pope would take the initiative to contact a Protestant Pentecostal pastor and then invite himself to that Protestant church in order to acknowledge wrongs and publicly ask forgiveness. This event was deeply impactful, historic, and unprecedented, and is one of the signposts that the John 17 Movement is not about a merger or erasure of Christian denominations and groups. Rather, it is a recognition that we all serve the Lord Jesus Christ, and that when one group offends another group, no matter who it is, forgiveness needs to be offered and received for what has transpired. This is the foundation for all true reconciliation, and the basis for what is happening in the John 17 Movement.

Approximately nine months after this profound historic event, Mary and I were asked to join a trip to Rome to meet and participate in a Q&A with Pope Francis. To think we could participate in another historical event where a small group of Protestant pastors and leaders would sit down with the leader of the Roman Catholic Church and ask him biblical and philosophical questions was astounding for us to even contemplate. Three months later, we found ourselves en route to Rome, via Caserta, so we could first visit the home and church of Giovanni and Franca Traettino, where Pope Francis had visited a year earlier.

After this remarkable experience in Caserta, we traveled to Rome to gather with the John 17 group, so we could meet together prior to having an audience with Pope Francis. One of the preparatory meetings was with the person arranging the meeting, Julia Torres, who explained what would happen the next day when we met with him. She explicitly explained the main reason for her meeting with us was to tell

us about the "man," the person she had known for over two
decades before he became Pope Francis. She shared their history and communicated the human side of Pope Francis and
how his personal relationship with Christ and his passion
to see Christ's Church healed was the reason we were able
to see him. Since the Kingdom of God is first and foremost
relational and moves forward at the speed of relationship, he
wanted to personally relate to us by spending time getting
to know us.

When Julia found out that Mary worked as a speech
therapist in a private Catholic school in our community, she
offered to provide a set of rosaries for each employee as a
personal gift from Pope Francis. Mary was deeply touched
by her gracious offer, especially in light of the preparations
Julia was already handling for the meeting the following day.

Words are insufficient for Mary and I to fully convey
the depth and breadth of impact we experienced when we
were privileged to meet with Pope Francis for over two hours
on that June day of 2016. Even our first impressions were
overwhelming, as he dismissed his security detail and asked
that only one Roman Catholic cardinal from the Vatican,
Cardinal Koch, remain with him while he answered questions from this predominantly Protestant group. His sincere
warmth and obvious charity were extremely disarming and
made us feel like he was a long-lost family member.

Following the brief greeting time, during which he gift-
ed each of us with a copy of his recent exhortation *The Joy
Of The Gospel*, we worshiped together. Seeing everyone lift
their voices and hearts as one to sing "I love you, Lord," including Pope Francis, worshiping the darling of heaven, was
emotional, and there were tears everywhere. For my wife
and I, ours were tears of repentance, as well as joy. We stood
there repenting over our attitude toward others in the Body
of Christ, especially Roman Catholics. Both of our families
are devout Catholics, and over the years we had developed
an attitude of spiritual pride that caused resentment among
our family members. And yet there were also tears of grati-

tude that we were standing there on this historic journey of relational reconciliation. Our hearts were immediately and miraculously enlarged to love more and walk closer with others from faith backgrounds that at one time we would have dismissed because of our narrow understanding of the diversity of the Body of Christ. Faith in Jesus Christ and his finished work on the cross is our common denominator, and we were choosing to focus on that, not on our differences. We felt the smile of our heavenly Father.

The wisdom and insight with which Pope Francis answered difficult biblical and philosophical questions was astonishing. As he graciously fielded our questions, some of which were controversial, he maintained his humor and candor, all the while providing cogent and biblically sound answers, often including biblical references and addresses. Several times after humbly providing incisive answers, Pope Francis would then say, "That's what I think; what do you think? What are your thoughts?" Even after the prepared questions were finished, Pope Francis looked at everyone and said, "Are there any other questions?" There were several, and when the questions were potentially affronting, he graciously responded with wit, candor, and his usual humor. We were enthralled.

What began as a trip to formally meet Pope Francis became an introduction to a new family member, one we never thought we would have the opportunity to meet. The experience exceeded our expectations in every way. Since spending this time with Pope Francis in Rome, we are even more committed to doing our part to help relational reconciliation and healing take place in the Body of Christ. True to her word, at the end of our visit, Julia gave Mary a box of Vatican rosaries, which were joyfully and incredulously received by Mary's grateful coworkers. To put it mildly, that act of kindness did much to further the spirit of unity in our community.

Between the incredible relational connection being established with John 17 and Pope Francis and what has taken place in the last twenty years in northern New York State, there is a renewed passion in our hearts to see the dream Jesus prayed in John chapter 17 actually become a reality: that his followers would "be one, as [he and the Father] are one" (verse 22). A unity not based on the lowest common denominator of our faith, but rather unity with diversity, where we sincerely respect each other's interpretations of scripture and choose to love one another even though there are differences in the non-essentials. Years ago when beginning the journey of unity in Massena we chose to adopt the famous adage Rupertus Meldenius penned in 1627: "In essentials, unity; in non-essentials, liberty; in all things, charity." In this light, we continue to practice supportive speech and actions toward each other and base our fellowship on scripture, Christ's love, and the historical Nicene Creed.

Although the John 17 Movement is certainly not the first of such unity movements in history, there appears to be a significant difference because of the depth of investment and personal commitment Pope Francis demonstrates with John 17. The energy, time, and vision he contributes to this movement indicate that unity is not simply an agenda item he is checking off, but rather a force in his life to help Christ's followers "become completely one" as Jesus and the Father are one.

If this is the future of the global Church in the months and years that lie ahead, we truly have something to look forward to as we discover the beauty, with all its diversity, of the Body of Christ.

Jesus, Our Peace

Gary Kinnaman

One of my best friends became Catholic. He would say he "converted to Catholicism."

What was he thinking?

Wayne spent most of his adult life in the church where I served as lead pastor for twenty-five years. We became close friends. I formally dedicated his children (in churches that only baptize adults, dedication is a kind of substitute for infant baptism). Wayne served as chairman of our church board, too, and to make things really personal, he's my financial advisor.

When Wayne "converted," many of his extended family followed him and became Catholic. They *all* had faithfully attended my church for years.

What happened? What did I do wrong?

My roots are Lutheran! You know, those are the people who pride themselves on starting the whole Protestant thing. After graduating from a Lutheran college, my non-Catholic perspective was reinforced by graduate degrees from Fuller Theological Seminary and Western Conservative Baptist Seminary.

Evangelical seminary-trained Gary and new Catholic Wayne. We have here a collision of two very different worlds. In the Bible, it might be like Jews and Gentiles. Or Jewish *Christians* and Gentile *Christians*. Across America, people of color and white people, followers of Fox News and those convinced NPR and CNN are telling the truth.

Yes, conservatives and liberals, men and women, even husbands and wives. In so many ways, we are worlds apart, where it's not just differences that divide us. It's our obsessive hostility over those differences. Every division, it seems, morphs into a life and death fight to the finish about who's right and who's wrong. You might even have to kill those people who are "wrong," which is the terrible side of human history, "Christian" history included.

What's a good Protestant to do when someone close to him "converts" to Catholicism? Well, don't you know, you have to exhaust yourself—and him—with endless arguments. You know he is *so* wrong and you are *so* right, and don't we all know that God is always on the side of those who are right. Somehow we've come to believe that our relationship with God is essentially about who is *most* right.

Putting right-and-wrong aside, how do we deal with rampant polarization and hostility over just about everything? We live in a culture of anger. Is there hope? Yes, indeed! But only as we *together* bring our differences to the foot of the cross. Paul says this so simply: "Be subject to one another out of reverence for Christ" (Ephesians 5:21). Our differences don't go away when we are together in the presence of Jesus, but the cross puts our sin, our self-centeredness, and our hostility to death.

This must be the centerpiece of every Christ follower:

> For he [Jesus] is our peace; in his flesh he has made both groups [hostile Jews and Gentiles or hostile _____ and _____] into one and has broken down the dividing wall, that is, the hostility between us . . . that he might create in himself one new humanity in place of the two, thus making peace, and might reconcile both groups to God in one body through the cross, thus putting to death their hostility through it. (Ephesians 2:14-16)

39

Jesus did this for us, for our whole hostile world, and he prayed for you and me in John chapter 17—and he continues to pray for us—to be one. And get this, he prays for us to be one *as he and the Father are one* (see verse 21). One. As the Father, Son, and Holy Spirit are *one* in the Holy Trinity. We are not just talking about agreements to be nice to each other even if we don't like each other. To be one as the three Persons of the Trinity are one is, well, mind-boggling.

I helped to facilitate a meeting of Christian leaders at odds with one another over ministry practices. The pastor leading the meeting began our time together with Holy Communion, the Eucharist. Our hope was that, by centering on the Person of Jesus, it would minimize our differences. It didn't. Even clergy can be hostile. One brother basically shouted, "We need true unity." *True* unity? What do you suppose he meant by that? I knew. He had his own definition of unity, and to have *true* unity, we had to agree to that definition. And it wasn't even about doctrine! It was about pastoral practice and style. It wasn't even distantly related to the unity of the Triune Godhead.

A soon as *we* define unity, unity vanishes, because how we define unity becomes more important than the Person who makes us one. Consider, instead, Paul's approach to the shamefully carnal and divided early Christian community in Corinth. "I decided," he declared, "to know *nothing* among you *except Jesus Christ*, and him crucified" (1 Corinthians 2:2, italics mine).

My deepest personal conviction is this: Our relationship with God is based on *Jesus plus nothing*, and that changes everything. In contrast, if we believe that God loves us, or another person, because of *Jesus plus something*, that "something" will always divide us.

The "something" may be a doctrine, a misunderstanding, a real difference, or something that's *really* important to us, like circumcision for the early Jewish Christians who believed with all their hearts, "Unless you are circumcised according to the custom of Moses, you cannot be saved" (Acts

15:1). To this the apostle Peter replied, "Why are you putting God to the test by placing on the neck of the disciples a yoke that neither our ancestors nor we have been able to bear? On the contrary, *we believe that we will be saved through the grace of the Lord Jesus*, just as they will" (Acts 15:10-11, italics mine).

What we believe and how we practice our faith are supremely important. Those things define us in a very personal way. It's what makes Catholics Catholic, Baptists Baptist, and Lutherans Lutheran. It's a large part of my identity— how I see myself, how I know myself, how I look at life, how I do life, what makes me unique.

And then Wayne has become a Catholic, and somehow, some way, that challenges who I am and what I believe. Wayne and I now no longer share in common some of the things that are most important in our respective lives. What keeps us together when we now have good reasons to drift apart? *Making Christ our center.* To find our ultimate identity in our relationship with the One who prayed for us to be one.

When we visited with Pope Francis in the summer of 2016, he said it this way: "We must make Jesus Christ our center, not the church."

Okay, so how are Wayne and I getting along now, ten years after he "converted"? Well, we don't go to the same church, but Wayne is still my financial advisor. But much more than that, we still thoroughly enjoy spending time together. Most importantly, in spite of our differences, we know we are brothers in Christ!

Recently, Wayne applied for admission to diaconate formation here in the Diocese of Phoenix. Outside of the Catholic Church, this would be a position something like an ordained lay minister. To be accepted, Wayne had to submit personal references, and he invited me, his non-Catholic former pastor, to write a good letter for him. I heard back from the director of the program how much he appreciated my support for Wayne!

But here's the best part of our story: the John 17 Movement, which has taken us to the Vatican to meet personally with Pope Francis, was born at the dinner table in Wayne's home! Like so many other ordinary moments in life, it began at a breakfast meeting I had with Wayne to talk about my retirement accounts. I told him I had met Auxiliary Bishop Nevares at an interfaith prayer breakfast, but subsequently I wasn't able to arrange a time to meet with him personally.

"I can make that happen!" Wayne announced confidently. "I know the bishop well, and we can have you both over to our home for dinner."

Meanwhile, Joseph Tosini's Italian friends Matteo Calisi (a Catholic leader) and Giovanni Traettino (a Pentecostal pastor) had made plans to visit Joseph in Phoenix. Matteo and Giovanni had led notable reconciliation gatherings in South America, which got Joseph to thinking about having them lead an evening service of worship and reconciliation in our city.

So when Joseph heard I was having dinner with Bishop Nevares, he did what only a good friend would do. He asked me for an invitation to our dinner with the bishop at Wayne's home. I called Wayne, he ran it by the bishop (and his own wife), and he let me know it would be great for Joseph and Mary to join us.

Over a wonderful Italian dinner and a glass or two of red wine, we talked about our shared relationship with Jesus and how Joseph had a dream of planting seeds of reconciliation in Phoenix. Filled with joy, Bishop Nevares lifted his hands and pleaded with us, "Can we just pray?!"

We did. We felt a deep sense of God's presence. We invited Bishop Olmsted into our "movement," and soon received a personal letter from Pope Francis letting us know he would be praying for our unity efforts in Phoenix! We believe these remarkable events are specific answers to our Lord's prayer for us to be one.

Yes, the Bible uses the term "unity," perhaps most notably in Ephesians 4:3: "Making every effort to maintain the unity of the Spirit in the bond of peace." Notice it doesn't say, "Maintain the unity *we create* for God." No, Paul is urging us to keep the *unity of the Spirit.* It isn't our business to make unity happen. It's our business to make every effort to honor and uphold what God gives us in Christ. Unity is never a human thing. It's always a God thing. Christian unity is transcendent, like the union of marriage.

Indeed, this is an image Paul uses to help us understand the Church and her relationship to Christ. He writes, "'For this reason a man will leave his father and mother and be joined to his wife, and *the two will become one flesh.' This is a great mystery*, and I am applying it to *Christ and the church*" (Ephesians 5:31-32, italics mine).

Married people don't just have unity. They become one without a single difference going away. The man becomes no less male, and the woman becomes no less female. It's the grand irony: differences attract, yet as most couples will tell us, marriage amplifies our differences. Life is conflicted, yet it's those frustrating and painful differences that invite us to live life on a deeper level, a life not merely of romance, but of sacrifice, of God-love: "Husbands, love your wives, just as Christ loved the church and gave himself up for her" (Ephesians 5:25).

With these thoughts in mind, consider this scripture again: "'For this reason a man will leave his father and mother and be joined to his wife, and the two will become one flesh.' This is a great mystery, and I am applying it to Christ and the church."

Look at these verses side by side:

"The two will become *one* flesh."

"Holy Father, protect them in your name that you have given me, *so that they may be one, as we are one*" (John 17:11, italics mine).

Our relationship with one another in the Body of Christ is not unlike marriage. We don't have to live together, but we do have to do life together with people we like, and with others we don't. So having a God-kind-of-love is the only pathway to peace.

Can you grasp this? Can anyone? "Holy Father, protect them in your name that you have given me, *so that they may be one, as we are one.*" This is clearly not a call to functional unity, but a deep and transcendent oneness in all our relationships with one another.

It's a unity, a oneness possible only through the miracle-working love of God, love that's patient and kind. Love that pleads with God to forgive us our sins as we forgive those who sin against us.

So who converted to Catholicism in your circle of life? Or left the Catholic Church because they were so transformed by what they heard from some preacher on TV?

Is Jesus able to give you love for the most difficult people in your life? No one likes to hear this, but few can disagree: God loves the worst people in your life more than you love the people you love the most.

Jesus, Son of God, have mercy on us. Keep praying for us to be one. We know you will work miracles among us to make that happen. Amen.

A New Creation

Bishop Eduardo Nevares

In 1981, I was ordained a Roman Catholic priest and missioned to a small town in East Texas. At that time, the Catholic population there was about 3%. I was in the middle of what has been known as the "Bible Belt." This means, among other things, that the Baptist denomination, as well as the Church of Christ and other Protestant denominations, dominated the television and radio stations with Christian programming.

When I arrived at my assignment, there was a Baptist Spanish-speaking pastor who had been in town for about five years. He was a former Catholic, and was now very anti-Catholic. He had a weekly radio program where he would lambast the Catholic Church as the "whore of Babylon" and the pope as the "antichrist," as well as the other typical criticisms. Some parish members encouraged me to begin a Roman Catholic radio program where I would be able to present the teachings of the Catholic faith. This I did, and shortly thereafter the pastor and I got involved in a type of "slug fest." What he said one week, I would respond to the following week, and what I said one week, he would respond to the following week. Of course, each of us would justify our faith positions using different quotes from the same Bible.

This back and forth, tearing each other's Church's teachings apart, was enjoyed by our congregations like a weekly boxing match. One week, the pastor would "win"; the other week, I would "win." This behavior caused great spiritual harm to me. I grew more and more angry with the Baptist preacher. I became more and more entrenched in my Catholic righteousness, and saw him as my enemy. Over time, I even began to see him as the devil. I was more determined than ever to continue espousing the Catholic "truths" to defend *my* parishioners from his lies and vile attacks.

This unchristian behavior between the pastor and myself also affected the families of our congregations in a negative way. There were many families in the town where some members were Baptist and others were Roman Catholic. There began to be more arguing and heated discussions among family members concerning their different faith beliefs. The parents also reported that the Catholic children were experiencing harassment at the public schools because of their faith.

The behavior of the faith "leaders" was scandalous. I was not setting a good example of the gospel values that Jesus Christ had taught. How could I get up week after week to preach the wonderful lessons on the love of God and neighbor in the Bible, and then show such disrespect and dishonor to the preacher's Baptist faith? My parishioners began to notice that my behavior toward the Baptist preacher during my radio program on Friday was not in keeping with the gospel that I preached on Sunday.

One day during my personal prayer time, I opened the Bible to the crucifixion scene. I meditated on everything that the Lord, Jesus Christ, had suffered for my sins and those of the whole world. After all that he had been through, he prayed, "Father, forgive them; for they do not know what they are doing" (Luke 23:34). The Lord brought the Baptist preacher to mind. He let me know that God has forgiven him all his vile behavior toward the Catholic Church. Jesus asked me, "Can you forgive?" I was deeply touched. I wept tears of repentance. I begged the Lord to forgive me for my pride, my anger, my hateful feelings, and the damage that I had done to my congregation. Then the Lord showed me the parable of the Good Samaritan. He showed me the Baptist preacher as the man beaten and left for dead. The Lord revealed to me some of the hurt and trauma that seminary professors had caused the preacher. I came to understand some of the reasons why he was so anti-Catholic.

Jesus told me, "The priest saw the man beaten, and passed by." He asked, "Will you continue to ignore his pain and his wounds, or will you be a good Samaritan to him?" I inquired, "Lord, what would you have me do?" The Lord answered, "Invite him for a cup of coffee." My immediate reaction was, "You've got to be kidding. Lord, the Baptist preacher has spoken terrible things against your Church, the pope, the Virgin Mary, and even myself. He is a liar, a scoundrel. If I have a cup of coffee with him, my parishioners will find out, and the Baptist parishioners will know that their pastor has finally 'won' the 'religious war' between us. All will know that I went groveling to meet him. I will be so shame-faced before my congregation." The Lord spoke abundantly clearly as he brought to my mind St. Paul's admonition in 2 Corinthians 5:17-20:

> So if anyone is in Christ, there is a new creation: everything old has passed away; see, everything has become new! All this is from God, who reconciled us to himself through Christ, and has given us the ministry of reconciliation; that is, in Christ God was reconciling the world to himself, not counting their trespasses against them, and entrusting the message of reconciliation to us. So we are ambassadors for Christ, since God is making his appeal through us; we entreat you on behalf of Christ, be reconciled to God.

That very day I called the Baptist pastor on the phone and invited him for a cup of coffee. He was pleasant and happily accepted my invitation to meet at a local coffee shop. After two years of battling dogmas and doctrines of our respective faith traditions on our individual radio programs, I was meeting him for the first time. We both arrived at the location on time. He was a middle-aged man with a Spanish accent, dressed in a suit and tie with a Bible in his hand. I was dressed in a black suit with a Roman collar.

We greeted each other with a shake of the hand. We each ordered a cup of coffee. The atmosphere was tense. I began the conversation by thanking him for agreeing to meet with me. I also asked him about the large Bible he had brought. He told me that this was his family Bible that he had brought with him from Spain when he first arrived in East Texas. And so, the conversation developed. No discussions of theology or philosophy. No dogmas or doctrines. We shared our family histories and stories, our common love for the Lord Jesus Christ, and some of our varied ministerial experiences. After two hours, the pastor offered to buy me supper. This kind gesture sealed our new friendship in the Lord.

As I drove home, I found myself rejoicing in the Lord. I felt a heavy burden lifted from my soul. So much negativity, so much anger, so much hatred, so much guilt over my treatment of my Baptist brother had been released, and I found myself singing, "Rejoice in the Lord always; again I will say, Rejoice" (Philippians 4:4). How blind I had been. How stubborn of heart. How slow to believe the instruction of the Lord to love our enemies (cf. Luke 6:27). I was humbled by the Lord to understand that even I, an ordained priest of God, was a sinner.

After this initial contact with the Baptist preacher, we did stop feuding on our radio programs. We continued to speak about our individual faiths and reasons for our individual practices, but we no longer criticized each other's faith traditions or Church.

With this experience in mind, I reread the document of Vatican Council II (1962-1965) known as the *Decree on Ecumenism*, on the restoring of Christian unity. In paragraph 7, I read: "There can be no ecumenism worthy of the name without a change of heart." The Council Fathers quoted St. Paul, the Apostle to the Gentiles:

I therefore, the prisoner in the Lord, beg you
to lead a life worthy of the calling to which you
have been called, with all humility and gentle-
ness, with patience, bearing with one another in
love, making every effort to maintain the unity
of the Spirit in the bond of peace. (Ephesians
4:1-3)

In 1 Corinthians 12:4-6, St. Paul says clearly, "there
are varieties of gifts, but the same Spirit; and there are varieties of services, but the same Lord; and there are varieties
of activities, but it is the same God who activates all of them
in everyone." A little further down, he continues:

For just as the body is one and has many members, and all the members of the body, though
many, are one body, so it is with Christ. For in
the one Spirit we were all baptized into one
body—Jews or Greeks, slaves or free—and we
were all made to drink of one Spirit. (1 Corinthians 12:12-13)

With this new vision of ecumenism, I began reaching
out to the other local Christian churches and their pastors.
Some were agreeable to meeting, and to share some Christian prayer times and activities together. We began having
an ecumenical prayer service during the Thanksgiving holi-
day season. During the Christmas season, we would provide
blankets and food for the elderly and the poor, as well as
toys for needy children. These Christian charitable activities continued for the several years that I was the Catholic pastor in town. Yet, after our Christian action events,
each pastor or priest would go back to his or her Christian
congregation, and continue taking care of their respective
congregants. There developed a respect and a friendliness
among some of the Christian denominations, yet there did
not seem to be that love that would unite us as brothers and
sisters in the Lord.

The unity of the Christian Church received new impetus with the election of Pope Francis in 2013. Following the spirit and directives of the Second Vatican Council, the new pope began reaching out to all people of good will. He has visited with Buddhist monks, Muslim imams, rabbis, and many bishops, priests, and ministers of the gospel of different Christian denominations. Pope Francis seems to have a heart-to-heart conversation with each of these faith representatives. He does not look upon them in an adversarial relationship but considers all to be his brothers and sisters.

The Holy Father has a fresh approach to ecumenism. Before, the dialogue between the Christian Churches was usually between the theologians. They would meet on occasion and discuss the meaning of the literary forms and words in the original languages of scripture. They would discuss the historical environments and situations from which each of the books of scripture were developed, and inform each other as to how each of their faith traditions had interpreted certain sections of the Bible. The Holy Father has thanked the theologians for their important and tedious work.

The pope has also, however, encouraged a much more "normal" or "human" manner of ecumenism. He has asked us Catholics to engage our separated brothers and sisters of other faith traditions by inviting them to a gelato or cup of coffee. It is in this accompaniment that ecumenism is not theorized and discussed, but lived and experienced. It is in this environment of friendship that we come to know and to discover that we are brothers and sisters in the risen Christ.

Pope Francis has also spoken of the "ecumenism of blood." He has mentioned that in the Middle East, Africa, Asia, and elsewhere throughout the world large populations of Christians are persecuted and even murdered for their faith. We have seen ISIS, for example, seek out Christians in every village that they terrorize. As they go from door to door, the terrorists do not ask, "Are you a Catholic Christian? Are you an Anglican Christian? Are you an Orthodox Christian? Are you an Evangelical Christian?" No. They simply ask, "Are you a Christian?" In many instances, if the person is a Christian, and has the courage to die for Christ, "the witness to Christ, even to the shedding of blood, has become a shared experience."[6]

Finally, the Holy Father has reminded us that as baptized Christians, all of us make up the one Body of Christ. Each of the individual church communities contributes charisms that help to build up the Kingdom of God. As we dialogue and visit with one another, we come to develop a relational ecumenism. We come to better understand one another's faith traditions. In this way, we come to experience the unity of which St. Paul speaks in Ephesians chapter 4.

I find it significant to remember that in the Vatican II *Decree on Ecumenism*, in paragraphs 3-4, the "Protestant" label for those who worship in other Christian communions has been changed to "separated brethren." The Holy Spirit is truly calling the Christian Churches to be reconciled to God and to one another, because of our sharing a common baptism into the one Body of Christ. Yes, there continue to exist many theological, philosophical, historical, dogmatic, and doctrinal separations. Yet, if we can approach our separated brothers and sisters as participating with us to some degree in the life of the Holy Spirit, and accentuate that which unites us, instead of that which divides us, I believe that we will be living that accompaniment which Pope Francis invites us to live.

I am very happy to end my reflection on the unity of the Body of Christ with another very real experience of the presence of the Holy Spirit. It happened when I met with two Christian pastors one evening for supper, Pastor Gary Kinneman and Pastor Joseph Tosini and their wives. We were all invited to the home of Gary's friends Wayne and Lisa in Phoenix, Arizona.

---

6. "Message of His Holiness Pope Francis on the Occasion of the Global Christian Forum [Tirana, 2-4 November 2015]," https://w2.vatican.va/content/francesco/en/messages/pont-messages/2015/documents/papa-francesco_20151102_messaggio-global-christian-forum.html.

We had a very nice dinner, with a tremendous sharing of our personal histories, our extensive ministerial experiences, and our common love of the Lord Jesus. As the supper was ending, I asked the group if we could gather to pray. I wanted to thank God for bringing us together, and for helping me to discover my new brothers and sisters in Jesus Christ.

We prayed for a few minutes. Then we sang some praise and worship songs. We were enjoying the presence of the Holy Spirit and felt the promise of Jesus fulfilled, "For where two or three are gathered in my name, I am there among them" (Matthew 18:20). We continued praying for another few minutes, when suddenly, the presence of the Holy Spirit became palpable, and from my mouth came forth the prayer of Jesus himself:

> . . . that they may all be one. As you, Father, are in me and I am in you, may they also be in us, so that the world may believe that you have sent me. The glory that you have given me I have given them, so that they may be one, as we are one, I in them and you in me, that they may become completely one, so that the world may know that you have sent me and have loved them even as you have loved me. (John 17:21-23)

I had read this passage from the high priestly prayer of Jesus to his heavenly Father many times. Yet never had I experienced this prayer lived in this concrete situation with a Pentecostal brother and sister and an Evangelical brother and sister. Here, before our very eyes, we were living the heartfelt prayer of Jesus to his Father. We heard, not with our ears, but with our hearts, this call of Jesus to unify his Body, the Church. Never had I understood that the little word *as* was so significant in the desire of Jesus. Jesus does not want our unity to exist only with a cup of coffee, nor with a dinner, nor with an occasional prayer service or work of charity. He wants the unity of his followers to be the unity that exists *as* in the blessed Trinity itself.

After 1,000 years of division between the Roman Catholic and the Eastern Orthodox Churches, and after 500 years since the separation of the Reformation Christian Communities, the Holy Spirit is once again offering to the Christian Church a new Pentecost, "so that the world may believe." Could it be that so many young people today, millennials and others under the age of thirty, are leaving Christian Churches because, even though we are good preachers, the witness of our lives does not convince them?

For the past four years, Pastors Tosini and Kinneman and myself, along with several other Christian brothers and sisters, have continued to preach and to live lives founded on the good news of Jesus Christ as seen in John chapter 17. In fact, the Holy Spirit has encouraged us to continue to meet, and to share our hopes and dreams for this unity of the Body of Christ that we have experienced. Thanks be to the Father, and to the Son, and to the Holy Spirit, we now have persons praying for this unity in Phoenix, Seattle, Houston, New York, and in many places throughout the world.

The John 17 Movement has had the support and encouragement of our Holy Father, Pope Francis, from the very beginning. He has written letters of support for our ecumenical encounters. When John 17 had its first citywide gathering in Phoenix, the Holy Father sent a nine-minute video, assuring us of his presence and sending his prayerful support. Some members of the movement were also blessed to be invited by the Holy Father to visit him at the Vatican for two consecutive years. A group of thirty to forty bishops, priests, pastors, and lay faithful have visited with the Holy Father each time. We have prayed together, we have sung the praises of the Lord together, and Pope Francis has shared with us encouraging messages and provided us with a very generous time for photographs.

All of us who have visited with the pope have been deeply touched by his simplicity, humility, humanity, and generosity. One of the Evangelical pastors came back to Phoenix and mentioned this trip to his congregation the following Sunday. After the service, one of his congregants approached him and asked, "Pastor, how was it to meet the antichrist?" The pastor responded, "I discovered that he is a brother in Christ."

Whenever we have a citywide John 17 Movement gathering, I have a glimpse of what heaven will be. There we are: the poor and the sick, the rich and the strong, the young and the seasoned, and representatives from different races and ethnic groups. Yes, children of one God and Father. As we pray, as we ponder the Word of God together, as we sing our spiritual songs to God, I cannot help but be reminded of the old African American spiritual "When the Saints Go Marching In": "Lord, how I want to be in that number, When the saints go marching in."

Friends in Christ

Bishop Thomas J. Olmsted

I had never met Joseph Tosini, but he made an offer I couldn't refuse. Joseph and others, mostly Evangelical pastors from Phoenix, were welcoming some guests from Italy, who brought a message from Pope Francis. "Would you have time to meet with us?" Joseph asked. An unexpected opening in my calendar made it possible for me to say yes. That yes opened a door to many blessings.

The letter from Pope Francis made clear his keen interest in the John 17 Movement, an interest sparked by his own friendship with Evangelical Christians like Giovanni Traettino, who came to Phoenix for that first meeting.

For many years, the prayer of Jesus at the Last Supper has resounded in my own heart: "That they may all be one. As you, Father, are in me and I am in you" (John 17:21). In part, this longing for unity in Christ stems from my love for my non-Catholic grandfather and anti-Catholic grandmother.

That powerful prayer of our Savior also deeply moved St. John Paul II, with whom I worked closely for nearly ten years and who has been a spiritual father for me. In him, I witnessed a deep commitment to pray and make special efforts to promote unity among all the baptized.

From the beginning of my participation in John 17, I have been warmly welcomed as a brother in Christ and invited to share my own story of coming to love the Lord Jesus and to join others in giving thanks and praise to God.

It has been moving to witness the personal love for Christ so evident in my Evangelical brothers and sisters, and to see their desire to build bonds of fraternity and friendship in fidelity to the prayer of Jesus. While I am not sure of the path that lies ahead, I trust that the Holy Spirit is the origin of this initiative and that he will bring forth good fruit if we faithfully follow his lead.

I trust that the good relationships that have been forged since the beginning of John 17 will continue to grow and that we will experience in still deeper ways the reality of Jesus' words at the Last Supper, "I do not call you servants any longer . . . I have called you friends" (John 15:15). I hope that the Holy Spirit, who has led us to take to heart Jesus' prayer in John chapter 17, will lead us also to complete unity in his name.

New Brothers and Sisters

Sharon and Peter Poppleton

The seeds of Christian unity were planted in us during July 1977. Sharon and Peter had met when they shared a ride to a retreat. Since their relationship started to grow, Sharon sent Peter a letter wanting an opinion on whether to go to the Kansas City Charismatic Conference with her prayer group. Peter thought it was a good idea, and Sharon accompanied her group to what would become a deep moment in the unfolding history of Christian unity.

Sharon

"Why can Protestants go into a Catholic church but Catholics can't go into a Protestant church?" The parish priest gave us one week to come up with the answer in the parochial school religion class. This was 1962. At age twelve, and the oldest of six children from a devout Catholic family, I really knew my Baltimore Catechism and was sure I could figure this out. There must be some profound theological reason that I just wasn't able to understand. After all, we were all Christians. I couldn't wait to hear the explanation. But we were told, "Because you aren't allowed to. It's a sin." Gosh, that's the answer? So much for my first foray into unity and ecumenism.

    The Second Vatican Council opened that very year and the Holy Spirit opened the doors to renewal and a new release of the "truth of the gospel" and clear encouragement of the work of ecumenism, although I personally wouldn't experience this for several more years.

The church of my childhood was changing and so was the entire culture—it was the sixties. The year 1968 in particular was a year of cultural rupture, embodied in protests by university students and others challenging current political and social values and aims. During the next few years, it seemed my whole family ruptured as well. Almost all of us stopped going to church. Miraculously, within a few years, all of us were back in church, but in very different ways. One of my sisters, somewhat a child of the sixties, experienced an encounter with Jesus as her Lord and Savior. One by one, she witnessed to us and all but one in the family came to the Lord: Three joined non-denominational churches and I and one other sister remained Catholic. My parents seemed to be both.

I had responded to an altar call in an Assemblies of God Church in Riverside, California, in July 1974. A week later, I received the Baptism of the Holy Spirit at the 1974 Catholic Charismatic Western Regional Conference in San Diego. I joined a Catholic prayer group in Hemet, California, where I was living at the time, studied the Bible with non-Catholics as well as Catholics, and basically hopped all around Southern California with many others getting "fed" (a common idiom in the early charismatic renewal days). There was a precious unity in the Spirit, whatever your background or denomination; you just wanted to be with others who had encountered Jesus as Lord and Savior.

Perhaps the apex of this unity manifested itself in the 1977 Kansas City Conference on Charismatic Renewal in Christian Churches. For five days over forty-five thousand believers from many denominations gathered: almost all the mainline Protestant Churches, Messianic and Born-Again Jews, Evangelicals, and non-denominationals. During the days, each group had its own series of teachings. I attended Catholic workshops as well as several non-denominational ones and one Messianic Jewish session. In the evenings, everyone gathered in Arrowhead Stadium for worship together and on the final night we cried together in glory that "Jesus is Lord." It seemed that the Kingdom of Heaven was just about here—we were truly one in the Spirit. To use a Catholic analogy, it was almost as though an indelible mark for ecumenism was put on my soul during that worship session. Everyone I've ever spoken to who attended the conference had a similar experience.

Along with the experience of joy, we were sobered by words spoken through several prophets on the last day. One that came through Ralph Martin seemed to remind us that the unity of the Body of Christ still had a long way to go: "Mourn and weep, for the Body of My Son is broken! . . . Come before me with broken hearts and contrite spirits . . . with sackcloth and ashes! I would have made you one new man, . . . a light on a mountaintop. . . . My people are scattered. . . . The Body of My Son is broken!"[7]

My husband Peter and I married five months after the conference. We discerned the Lord calling us to serve the renewal of the Catholic Church in a covenant community. We have been members of City of the Lord, a Catholic Charismatic Covenant Community and founding member of the Catholic Fraternity of Charismatic Covenant Communities and Fellowships, for forty years. Initially, we were an ecumenical community, consisting of about 94 percent Roman Catholics and a minority from other churches. In 1989, there was a unanimous vote to become a Catholic community. This was sad in that our hearts longed for unity; it was good in that we could freely talk in prayer meetings with our own "lingo" and experience our liturgical life together as well as charismatic worship.

My family lives all over the United States, from Florida to Seattle, but often engages in fellowship with monthly

---

7. "Prophecies from the Kansas City Ecumenical Conference in 1977," New Life Charismatic Renewal Ministry, accessed April 17, 2018. http://newlifecrm.org/newsletters/Prophecy.htm.

prayer conference calls. These have not always been easy for me, in that if I mentioned anything overtly Catholic, such as the wisdom of a particular saint on an issue, an awkward silence usually followed. I learned to relate at the lowest common denominator of faith expression. However, in recent years, this tension has significantly decreased, with there being a much greater acceptance of each other's differences. I see in this a movement of the Holy Spirit for ecumenism in our hearts.

Ecumenism within the John 17 Movement plays out often as an exchange of gifts, and an appreciation of what the other has to offer. For example, a few years ago, about fifteen of us attended a small retreat in Shorum, Long Island. Three of us were Catholics. Before lunch one day, an Evangelical pastor said, "Let's say the Sign of the Cross in honor of our Catholic brethren." I never experienced anything like this forty years ago. Of course, there is always a need for sensitivity in this exchange; I wouldn't mention my beliefs about Purgatory or suggest prayers from Catholic devotional sources in an ecumenical setting. Together we focus on what is held in common, but there is an acceptance of how the Lord has worked in each in different ways, as I witnessed on the Shorum retreat.

Another instance of this mutual regard is the long and beautiful conversation Peter and I had with a Pentecostal pastor about our different understandings of Eucharist. There was no effort on either side to convince the other of his or her "truth." It was a time of getting acquainted with each other as formerly "separated brethren" longing for oneness in the Lord whom we no longer wished to grieve. There are, of course, times and places for these types of discussions. But my experiences in John 17 are all about getting to know each other, learning to care for each other, and having a good time in the Lord together.

For decades I had a sorrow in my heart that the glories of the Kansas City conference hadn't continued. I could not and would not ever forget Kansas City, but I came to think of it as a distant vision that I would not see come to pass. What went wrong? Some say egos and pride got in the way. But perhaps the seeds planted forty years before had simply been dormant and were waiting to sprout when mature. I could never forget the cry of the Father's heart for unity among his children that I heard in 1977. With the first gatherings of the John 17 Movement a few years ago, I almost cried from joy. Could now be the time for the vision? Perhaps we have been broken and humbled to the point where each can say, "Yes, Lord, we want unity your way, not my way. Please, Lord, help us to not wound your heart again. Help us get it right. And so, we pray together, 'In your mercy, pour your grace upon us once more, that united in Spirit we can cry out together, Jesus is Lord.'"

Peter

It is now July 2013. Sharon and I arrive at Lake Junaluska and join the Alleluia Ecumenical Covenant Community in the celebration of their fortieth anniversary. There are many brothers and sisters we do not know, though we are greeted and caught up into their celebration. We feel like privileged guests amid the excitement of the weekend.

The path to this celebration began earlier in the year when I assumed the role of overall coordinator of City of the Lord, a Catholic Covenant Community. Both Alleluia and City of the Lord share a common heritage, although Alleluia answered the call to be an ecumenical community and City of the Lord answered the call to be fully Catholic. As we entered the celebration time, the difference in the calls created some inner tension within me, especially since some members of City of the Lord hoped that my background would be helpful in bringing our community into a fuller expression of the Christian faith as Roman Catholics.

Sharon and I both came from Catholic homes; when we met we both returned to active participation in our faith. We raised our three sons in a rich Catholic culture celebrating the multiple dimensions of our faith, visiting Rome, and even personally meeting Pope St. John Paul II at Castel Gandolfo. Plus, for the previous thirty-plus years I had worked in product development, marketing, and sales for several Catholic religious education publishers. This professional position brought me further into the Roman Catholic faith. I worked with parishes, parochial schools, and dioceses. A major goal was to increase product lines in parishes, but I also had a strong desire to serve the Roman Catholic Church. It was no surprise, then, that I arrived at Lake Junaluska with my interior "Catholic clothes" on.

On the first evening of the celebration Sharon and I were invited to a social gathering of leaders. We were in the midst of an ecumenical event along with leaders and guests from different faith traditions. My head was trying to process the meaning of the intersection of two different communities. My mind was filled with theology, sacraments, etc., and swirling Catholic ideas filled my head with a tension to which I was not accustomed. *These are brothers and sisters?* So I put a cordial smile on my face and I met the leaders and guests from different faith traditions.

At one point I stepped back a bit into a corner—maybe both literally and figuratively. I looked around the room. A quieting thought came to mind: *Yes, these are my brothers and sisters in the Lord. Hm.* This thought seemed to open a door in my heart which began, literally, to grow very warm. My mind did indeed quiet down as the warmth in my heart increased. The cordial smile on my face became genuine.

My Catholic faith was not dismissed. If anything, it was expanded. I saw the brothers and sisters in the room through a new set of eyes. These eyes rose up from my heart and offered an ecumenical way of seeing the broader Church where Jesus Christ is truly Lord! As the evening unfolded I observed that Sharon was very busy in lively conversations. She seemed very comfortable and must not have needed the process that had brought me peace. At one point both of us were sitting in conversation with Lutheran pastor Larry

Christenson and his wife Nordis. Pastor Christenson was a pioneer in the charismatic renewal movement. We knew of his books and felt privileged to be speaking with them. Before the evening ended I invited him to be a guest speaker at one of the Sunday gatherings of City of the Lord in Phoenix.

Sharon and I had been pulled into an amazing grace-filled moment. Little did I know that within six months I would meet the Catholic bishop of Phoenix at the first ecumenical gathering of John 17. The bishop would walk up to me and say, "Peter, I want you and City of the Lord to be involved with this group known as John 17." The ecumenical current of grace picked me up and brought me into a place totally unexpected in order to participate in one of the movements of unity within the broader Body of Christ.

For Peter and Sharon, the decisive beginning in Kansas and the movement in the heart at Lake Junaluska found further expression in John 17. May the many graces of this historical time encourage more of us to allow the Lord to bring us from our heads into our hearts for purposes we may not fully understand but which, in the Lord, will bear fruit for his Kingdom.

A Humble and Welcoming Shepherd

Joshua Butler

I am a pastor and author in Portland, Oregon. My wife Holly and I were honored to have the unique opportunity to meet Pope Francis. Prior to this, I had believed in Church unity, had a positive respect and appreciation for the Catholic faith, and read Catholic theologians and authors who informed my own journey with Jesus. But this trip sparked a new passion to be more proactive at working toward relational unity with churches in Portland.

I want to share some highlights from our group's conversation with the pope. Pope Francis introduced the time and welcomed those present as "brothers and sisters," for when we confess Jesus as Lord and are united, he observed, the Lord is present in our midst: "And I believe the Lord is here today." He invited us to simply talk like friends, comparing our gathering for conversation to a game of soccer: "the ball is in the middle—somebody take the ball!"

The Uniqueness of Jesus

We first asked Pope Francis about the uniqueness of Christ: what makes Jesus unique, and how do we articulate that as his followers today? He chuckled and responded in his typical fashion, simple yet profound: "Jesus Christ is unique because he is the only Lord." Jesus has all authority and rules the earth, he continued, yet he rules in sacrificial love. As Christians, when we want to express Christ to the world, we need to make love concrete. Sometimes our actions can be more powerful than our words.

This is also relevant to our unity as Christians. What do we share in common? We are the people of Jesus. There is great diversity in the Church, but what holds us together, Paul tells us, is "one Lord, one faith, one baptism" (Ephesians 4:5). These are the things that unite us, said the pope, and though they are only a few simple things they bring our great diversity together in the power of Jesus' Spirit as his people.

Mission

One of my questions was about the mission of the Church and the role of the laity (people in the church who are not priests or clergy). Pope Francis lit up with excitement to talk about this and said this is the sense of the "synodality" of the Church, which begins in the local parishes. "I told a gathering of bishops in Latin America," he said, that "clericalism is one of the biggest problems in the Church."

Clericalism is the situation when the people of the church exist to support the clergy, he explained, rather than the clergy existing to serve and build up the church and its people. Laypeople, through their baptism into the Church, have a mission. They are not there to serve the priest; they themselves have the voice of the Spirit in the Church. Clericalism has not helped the Church grow, and we need to go deeper in reclaiming the centrality of the laity in the Church.

When I think of clericalism, he said, I think of Eli in the Bible. He referred to the story in 1 Samuel chapter 1, basically saying Eli suffered from clericalism, but Hannah, as a representative of the everyday people of God, was able to move Eli's heart as a priest to contribute to God's redemptive movement in the world.

Humility

The pope talked about how the Church needs to continually be called back to the feet of its Lord, at one point saying, "A Church with no prophets is a dead Church." I am struck by how Francis has lived out this "prophetic humility," as I've learned how some of his first acts as pope were to fire many powerful figures known for corruption, worldliness, and arrogance. The new pope also officially renounced the mafia and replaced many prominent advisors and staff of the Vatican financial institute.

He's been cleaning house—or as he put it, "flipping the omelet." Yet he walks with a bold humility, with a seemingly impenetrable joy in the midst of what must be monumental pressures and expectations surrounding him, and a clarity of seeking Jesus' voice and calling all who will come to join him at the feet of Jesus.

Pope Francis's humility was evident throughout the conversation. When it opened, for example, he was seated in a larger chair set out a little at the front and center of the room, and one of his first comments was, "I wish I could just be sitting in one of your chairs there with you all." He would regularly say things like, "This is just me speaking. I don't want to be the teacher, I'm a pastor like you," which is pretty humbling coming from the pope.

Pope Francis asked for water at one point, and we all assumed it was for himself. Then we realized it was for the translator, who he figured must be thirsty. I think it's powerful that in the middle of this whole event, he was thinking of the translator. There seems to be a constant deflection in his words and actions to draw attention to Jesus and others instead of himself, to see his leadership as a call to serve the people rather than exalt himself over the people. It's a radical contrast to the ego and pride we see so often in the leadership culture of our world (including, sadly, the Church).

Funny Interlude

About an hour into our gathering, the moderator mentioned, "We probably only have a few more minutes," to which Pope Francis responded, "Why? Do you have to get the airport?" He'd been given an out, to get on with what I'm sure is a busy schedule, but it was a sign of his hospitality and generosity with his time that he brushed it off with a joke as if we were the ones needing to leave. We went on to talk for another hour or so.

Living in Tension

Another question I asked was how to be a faithful, prophetic witness amidst the political tensions of our divided culture. In the United States, our culture is divided and our political climate is tense, with many churches feeling pressure to become more partisan one direction or the other or to withdraw from the public square altogether—neither of which seem like faithfulness to Christ. Pope Francis responded, "Thanks to the Lord that there are tensions, because the Lord Jesus himself faced many tensions in his ministry."

He pointed to the four strong Jewish parties of Jesus' day—the Sadducees, Pharisees, Zealots, and Essenes—in addition, of course, to the all-powerful Romans. We see the spirit of the Zealots when James and John want to call down fire and destroy a city, while the Essenes were like spiritual monks, withdrawing from a corrupt society. Jesus lived in the tensions of that time, the pope explained, and it's wonderful to see the way he responds to the teacher of the Law who came to test him, or to the mother of John and James who wanted her children to climb in the reign of God, or to Judas.

"Where did Jesus live most of his life? On the street, and the tensions were there." The Lord would listen to everyone, but especially he was with the crowd, the poor, the weak. And we hear the tension in Gethsemane when he prayed to his Father, "If you are willing, remove this cup from me" (Luke 22:42). It's going too far to say he was "fighting" with his Father, the pope said, and of course Jesus also said, "Not my will but yours be done," but he was there in the tension.

"If a pastor is not feeling the tensions, it's because he's not living with his people. Instead, he is in a 'spiritual lab,'" Francis said. "If we feel the tension, it's because we're living in reality," like Jesus.

I was moved once again by how Pope Francis regularly brought everything back to Jesus. His response to most questions began by recalling a particular story about Jesus from the Gospels, or an attribute of Jesus described in the New Testament. It was inspiring to have the conversation repeatedly brought back to Jesus at the center.

"I Can't Live Without People"

Pope Francis has chosen not to live in the apostolic palace (a beautiful, ornate, historic residence where the pope usually lives), but rather in the Casa Santa Marta (a more humble, common living space with many others at the Vatican). We asked if he could share why he made this choice. This was a great setup for a humble-brag, but instead, he joked that a group of schoolchildren asked the same question when he first became Bishop of Rome, to which he humorously responded: "For psychiatric reasons."

Because he's a social person, he wanted to live somewhere with others, and with guests who come and go, to eat together and talk with them. The apostolic palace is historic and beautiful, he observed, and it would be unchristian and a shame if someone destroyed it out of a false sense of pride. So his decision "has nothing to do with proud reasons or going against anything for ideological reasons; [it's] simply because I'm not a 'cloister monk.' I can't live without people, it's a personal thing," he added, noting, "my mother made me like that."

Being closer to people also helps you govern better, he observed. A characteristic of a pastor should be closeness to the sheep (*pastor* literally means "shepherd"). The pastor doesn't leave the sheep alone when he goes to sleep; he is always with the sheep, always amongst the people.

After the gathering, Giovanni Traettini (a Pentecostal pastor in Italy and a good friend of Pope Francis) shared a funny Italian saying with me, "If you can't smell the stink of the sheep on their clothing, then they're not really a pastor." In an age of upward mobility and gated communities, when moving up in leadership often implies moving away from the messiness of those you lead, it's striking how Pope Francis lives out this "call to closeness," even if symbolically, at such a high level of leadership. He is seen regularly out with his people, hugging refugees and washing their feet, kissing the face of a disfigured man, listening to the questions of children, and looking folks in the eye as he shakes their hand.

The World Economy

Before becoming pope, Francis was archbishop of Buenos Aires. Now, having a broader scope of responsibility, we asked, how has your perspective on the world changed?

"At the center of the world economy, the very center, we no longer have man and woman as creatures of God, but rather money, the god money," Francis replied. "This is the great challenge: to place man and woman again at the center of humanity." Of course, work and business are not bad in themselves, he observed. Speaking technically, the market economy itself is not bad. But it should serve humanity, so that we share the richness the Creator has given to us all, and ensure the human being is not used.

The Tower of Babel is an illustrative example, he said, where the bricks were the "richness" of that time (because making a brick was difficult, with the mud, the straw, and the work to make it). It took a lot of work to make one brick, and stacking the bricks up high was a risky and difficult job. If the brick fell, it was a serious problem, and the one who dropped it was punished. But if one of the workers fell down, no problem. They would just carry that one away and replace them with another worker. Riches had replaced humans in value.

Similarly today, he said, if you find a human being, for example, a homeless person, dead in the square in Rome, it's no news. They just take him away and it's finished. But if the stock exchange goes down anywhere in the world, say, three points, it's a great calamity and it's all over the papers. It's the same thing as the bricks. "Man and woman are the great creation of God, at the center of creation," the pope stressed. Their increasing displacement by riches is the biggest change he's observed in the world these last four years; "or better yet," he nuanced, "it's my knowledge of the world that has changed."

The Power of Touch

We commented that the pope is famous for embracing people, shaking their hand, looking them in the eye. And he has said it's good not to just give something to the poor, but to touch them. We asked him to explain why that's important. "It's important because of Matthew chapter 25," Pope Francis said with an air of finality, as in: *Done. Problem solved. Next question.* Everyone laughed. But he continued, explaining that it's important because in the fullness of time God sent his Son, born of a woman. Jesus is God and man—and he identifies with the marginalized, saying what we've done to them is what we've done to him. The Word has incarnated into flesh, entering into our condition, and if somebody denies this, 1 John tells us, that person is the antichrist. God descended to us in his Son: he suffered, was betrayed, and was crucified for us. And now the marginalized who suffer, according to his words, are himself: "You did it to me."

"That's why I touch the flesh of the poor and don't have to be shy. I don't have to give the coin and take my hand back. I can look him in the eyes, because he's a human being." It's one thing to give money to help people, he said; this is a basic human thing to do. But it's something more to give love and charity. So a Christian can be human and give money to help. But a Christian *has* to touch the poor with love, because this is something Jesus Christ does for us, and because touching the flesh of the poor is touching Christ.

My Confession and Blessing

At the close of our Q&A time, I made a confession to the pope and received his blessing. I'd originally had other questions I wanted to ask that were more doctrinal in nature, but we'd talked about so many of those that, prayerfully in the moment, there was something else I wanted to say: "I have a confession to make." I said it a bit tongue-in-cheek, and the pope and everyone chuckled at the image of an Evangelical Protestant coming to confess to the pope. I went on to explain how in Portland we're blessed to be part of a network of around one hundred Evangelical churches working together to serve the city, in areas like caring for refugees, foster care and adoption, anti-trafficking, homelessness, and schools. And it has had a dramatic impact not only socially but also in displaying the love of Jesus in the city and a sense of the unity of the Church.

But my confession was that I have not worked hard enough to build bridges with our Catholic brothers and sisters in our city as part of the movement of the Body of Christ, and when I go back I want to be intentional about that. Francis got a large smile on his face and blessed me, saying: "The Lord will bless your efforts." It was a special moment, where God felt tangibly present. We ended by praying the Lord's Prayer, to *our* Father, all together.

The next year, I had the opportunity to return for a second gathering with Pope Francis, and was able to share an update. It has been exciting to see growing dialogue with Catholic and Evangelical brothers and sisters in Christ in our city. We invited the John 17 Movement to be part of a bridge-building and unity event we hosted in our city with a variety of churches. And this second year a cohort of us made the trip together, as Protestants and Catholics eager to continue working toward bridge-building at home. Our hope is that in many of the cities represented on this trip and beyond, it will be a catalyst toward similar relational unity work.

After the event, Pope Francis approached me with a smile beaming ear-to-ear on his face, and shook my hand, saying, "*Grazie* (Thank you), for your testimony!"

I was beaming ear-to-ear too . . . and when I think about it, I still kind of am.

Open to God's Heart

Linda Morris

For years I sat in my church and privately questioned the Lord about his real plans for my life and the lives of all who call themselves Christians. These questions came to mind periodically from the day I really met Jesus in February 1980 until today. Salvation placed within me a deep hunger to really know the heart of God. Therefore, my primary question has been, "Is this all there is to serving you?" I concluded that there had to be more to church and religion than church attendance, ushering, and singing. Surely, we are not saved to simply "ride the pew to heaven."

Whenever I have asked that question, God has faithfully provided life-changing experiences that alter my current direction and the course of my life. The question led me to Phoenix, Arizona, in 1983, when I became a member of the First Pentecostal Church. Twelve years later, the same question opened the door for me to travel and work in an Islamic country, where I learned to serve the Lord in a land where doing so was not acceptable. It was in that place that I glimpsed the *real* Church for the very first time. In that country, Christians were lumped together without denominational, doctrinal, or class divides. For this reason, we worshipped Jesus together and served the persecuted Church, others, and one another selflessly.

Upon my return to the United States, I was dismayed to realize that my out-of-country experience was not the reality at home. Once again, I asked the question. Our faithful God answered by providing employment in a mission-ori-

ented organization that developed lessons, taught incarnational and wholistic (having to do with the completeness of
the whole person as a child of God) ministry, and raised up
indigenous leaders in countries around the world to imple-
ment and demonstrate the heart of Jesus' teaching in practical ways. Christians in those countries began to love others
and serve them in ways that caused transformation and revelation of God's plan for his creation and his Church. True
wisdom is the word of God applied. James exhorts believers
to "be doers of the word, and not merely hearers" (1:22).
Yet, my homeland experience seemed to expect me to hear
the word and limit my "doing" to just being nice and ren-
dering benevolence to the less fortunate. As a follower of
Jesus, however, I believe my call is to do what Jesus did and
serve in my world as he served in his. So I was disappointed
to learn that the organization's ministry did not impact the
United States but was primarily focused on what it called
the "two-thirds" world.

I became a student of scripture and the lessons developed for the international audiences, and I longed to im-
plant this teaching in the United States. I resigned from my
position and became an unpaid volunteer to evangelize and
carry the incarnational wholistic ministry message, beginning at my own church. I was subsequently appointed outreach director for our church. In this capacity I am charged
to bring opportunities for the congregation to serve outside
of our assembly to show God's love to others. I knew that
I had to learn more from other churches and organizations,
so I began to network and serve at conferences and outreach
events outside of my local church, while recruiting members
to join me.

It was at one of these conferences that I met Joseph
Tosini, who I later learned was the founder of the John 17
Movement. During these encounters I began to see the
Church uniting as one family. I firmly believe from scripture
that there is only *one* Church and that mankind has divided
the Church that God intended to be a family.

Joseph and Mary invited my husband Burnett and me to a gathering at their home, and there I met Julia Torres. I shared a brief time of prayer with her, and our hearts knit together as I confessed that I had been praying for Pope Francis from the first day he was elected Bishop of Rome, because I believed I saw in him the humble but strong character of Jesus. I never thought I would go to Rome and *meet* Pope Francis! To this day I'm still amazed and must look at the photos to believe it really happened. After listening to Pope Francis's heart when we gathered in Rome, I realize that God is indeed reuniting his Church for all the world to see.

Today, as never before, I am committed to the ministry of reconciliation in and unification of the Body of Christ. There is a hunger in the Church for unity and for the Church to be relevant in the world today. I am eager to learn what God has in store as the Church becomes the Church of his heart.

In deep gratitude to the John 17 Movement leadership, I await the next direction from the Lord.

With Jesus' Eyes

Cal and Lisa Jernigan

"The eye is the lamp of the body. So, if your eye is healthy, your whole body will be full of light; but if your eye is unhealthy, your whole body will be full of darkness. If then the light in you is darkness, how great is the darkness!" (Matthew 6:22-23)

"One thing I do know, that though I was blind, now I see." (A man healed by Jesus, John 9:25)

Unity begins with the willingness to see the world through someone else's eyes.

It started with a simple invitation. Our friends Joseph and Mary Tosini invited us to travel to Rome with a small group of pastors, leaders, bishops, and priests to meet with the pope. We wondered, could this really happen? It was the invitation of a lifetime, and we knew it would bring forth a new responsibility and a sacred trust.

At the time, we were just beginning to understand the John 17 Movement and its relational approach for reconciliation within the Church at large, Protestants and Catholics. Though the movement was birthed with a focus on these two manifestations of one religious faith, its message extends way beyond these boundaries. John 17 is a learning lab for all faiths and an invitation for all people and all nations to enter into a dialogue of unity. We both sensed immediately God was calling us in.

For the past several years we have been engaged in the work of peacemaking. While there are lots of applications, we have especially been drawn to the Middle East, and most specifically, the Israeli-Palestinian conflict. This has not been an easy journey for us personally, or for our church. We have discovered, painfully, that peacemaking can be disruptive and unsettling for many. People would rather "keep the peace" (whatever that means) than work for and actually make peace in a broken and conflicted world. When you keep the peace you settle on silence, but when you engage as a peacemaker, you take it to a new level by leveraging your voice and speaking for those who cannot. The sad truth is that for a faith built on the teachings of "the Prince of Peace," many who follow Jesus aren't really interested in taking steps toward making peace. Making peace can be (and usually is) disorienting and discomforting, as you must enter into someone else's world and begin to see the world through their eyes and understand their "lens." It's far easier just to opt out and call it good.

Yet out of this conflict in the Holy Land we have seen God's Kingdom and his heart for the nations in new, convicting, and engaging ways. We have met with people in a posture of listening and learning, sitting in a variety of spaces: homes, refugee camps, settlements, churches, mosques, synagogues, and government offices; we have listened to people speak of unimaginable suffering and loss. We have also sat with the most amazing peacemakers who work tirelessly, believing peace is possible and worth the sacrifices.

> "Blessed are the peacemakers, for they will be called children of God." (Matthew 5:9)

Our journey of learning to live as everyday peacemakers has led us to ask ourselves some hard questions. One significant question is "How do we love the 'other'?" This is a question we are challenging ourselves and our church to understand and to live. Who is the other? The other is the one different than you—the one of a different faith, a different ethnicity, skin color, gender persuasion . . . There actually is no end to the number of "others" to be encountered. We are all so different when you think about it. The struggle is to learn how to love "the other" *because* they are different, not *in spite of* their difference. It is a journey that needs to be taken if we are ever going to usher in peace and unity and make a difference in this world.

As a couple, we don't want to settle just for what is, but rather live for something larger than ourselves. We believe we were made for more. We believe God is calling us to a place that is beyond our comprehension and that will ask us to give everything we have and are. Nothing less is worth living. This is why the invitation to join John 17 resonated and immediately grabbed our attention.

Our time in Rome was an "immeasurably more" experience on many levels. Meeting Pope Francis was surreal (yes, it really did happen!), but it went much, much deeper. It was not just meeting and being with the pope that was so impactful. It was more about being with the man behind the title and the clothes. While it conflicted with our Protestant preconceptions, we found him to truly embody everything Jesus. We say this not from a religious standpoint, but from a personal relationship. His heart for unity in the Body of Christ was abundantly evident.

We would like to share three specific highlights from our trip with you. Each of these left a mark on us and will not easily or soon be forgotten.

In the Vatican

The first highlight occurred in the meeting with Pope Francis in the Vatican. There, sequestered in a private conference room, we were privileged to engage in a two-hour question and answer period with him. This time began with him simply explaining to us that in football (soccer to Americans) you place a ball in the middle of the field, kick it around, and follow it wherever it goes. This was what he offered to us. He had no prepared speech, just a desire to dialogue with us. We were free to ask him whatever we wanted. We enthusiastically and fervently did so and he answered each and every question in a most gracious manner. While there is not time to elaborate on all the questions and report his responses, what neither of us will ever forget is how he, on a number of occasions, ended his response: with the simple comment, "Well, that's just my opinion, you're free to disagree." Somehow, we weren't raised to believe the pope says things like that. In this he was simply emphasizing his humanity and his desire to learn and grow. Be assured, Pope Francis truly is a humble man.

Unity is not about total agreement, but about entering into a dialogue to listen and learn without the need to debate. It is unity over uniformity. This is what we encountered in that sacred space with Pope Francis. He was not trying to convince us that one is right and the other (which we were, in that setting) was wrong. That wasn't the purpose or the desire of that gathering. It was space created for "friends" to gather in the name of Jesus and talk about what could be. What if we reframed our intentions and focused on our commonalities rather than our differences? What if the world would know us by our love for one another and not by our disagreements, hatred, division, and need to be right? Could unity prevail?

At Circus Maximus

The next two highlights took place inside the Circus Maximus, one of the first and largest stadiums in ancient Rome. The Circus Maximus hosted chariot racing, religious ceremonies, civic celebrations, and even gladiator fights. On this particular hot and humid day in June, it was the place where one hundred thousand Catholics gathered to be treated to a message by the pope (while over one million more joined in via the Internet). It was a celebration of the fiftieth anniversary of the Catholic Charismatic Renewal

Movement. Part of what was so moving about the event was the worship time that led off the celebration. If our eyes were closed, we wouldn't have been able to differentiate between what was happening there and what happens every week in our church back home. Yet this wasn't our tribe and we weren't theirs. This simply wasn't our tradition. Yet the same worship songs—songs sung with the same heart and spirit with which we sing them—were sung. To say this was eye-opening is an understatement. After a wonderful worship experience, the pope took to the platform and began his message.

He challenged the people in the crowd to follow Jesus, to submit to Jesus' will at every point in their lives. He talked about confession and repentance and the need to be baptized and to receive Jesus as their personal Lord and Savior. We were dumbfounded by the clarity and decisiveness of this message. We heard him say nothing that wouldn't be said to our people back home in our noticeably Protestant church. What made it even more surreal was the fact that there was a huge banner hanging on the stage behind him that declared, "Jesus is Lord." This was exactly the focus of his message and he couldn't have declared it any more clearly or profoundly.

The third highlight we want to share is while this entire program was going on, Pope Francis insisted that a number of us Evangelical pastors and leaders join him on the platform. This was his way of making a statement regarding our unity and oneness. Pastors and priests alike all joined together. So there Cal was, sitting on the stage with the pope, alongside a cadre of cardinals and a number of fellow pastors at one of the largest gatherings we have ever witnessed. What made this even more surreal (as if it needed something more) was that for the entire program Cal was seated directly behind the pope, just behind his left shoulder. What difference did this make? Cal says he will never have the opportunity to experience something through the eyes of the pope more closely than he did on that particular day. He watched as the people looked at Francis, and he watched how Francis looked at them. To say that he is revered by the masses is of course a supreme understatement; to say that he cares deeply about the masses was a lesson we'll never forget.

Afterward

As we've pondered this experience, we have come to realize that this really is what the heart of Jesus is all about. To be like Jesus we must come to see things the way he sees them, to look at people through his eyes. When Jesus said, "Love your enemies," it wasn't just a lofty platitude but a practical way to live our lives. When he taught us to forgive those who had wronged us, he knew that he would set the example while hanging from a cross. To look at the crowd who put him there, and then ask the Father to "forgive them; for they do not know what they are doing" (Luke 23:34). You see, it's one thing to tell people how to behave, how to respond, how to live; it's a whole different thing to then actually do it.

The John 17 Movement is based on Jesus' prayer as recorded in that book and chapter of the Bible. When we think of the text of John chapter 17 we can't help but be moved by the passion of Jesus. His prayer is intense; it is focused. Jesus' deepest desire is that the Church would not be broken into factions, but that it would be a unified whole. How his heart must grieve over what we have done to his Church! For the smallest of reasons we separate from one another and convince ourselves that this is exactly what Jesus would desire we do. How many factions of Christianity have we created? This should, in and of itself, be seen as something tragic. How much more so when we realize the one we all made a commitment to follow as our Lord and Savior specifically prayed that this not happen!

To change the course of history, someone has to take the lead. Part of what made this journey to Rome so incredibly significant for us was that it was ultimately at the invitation of Pope Francis. He initiated our visit by offering himself and his time to Joseph Tosini and his friends. He did this on the five hundredth anniversary of the birth of the Protestant Reformation. What must not be missed in all of this is the risk Pope Francis was willing to take by engaging John 17. He has just as much, or more, to lose, because many in his tribe think this is not wise or beneficial on his part. But who initiates peace? Here's what we've learned: the most secure and stable party in a dispute is always the one who makes the first move. They are the ones who place the value of the relationship as supreme and simply aren't content to let division reign. This is true in any disagreement in a marriage, and it is true on the world's stage. Secure people are not threatened by reconciliation; indeed, they recognize it as the only way forward.

> So that they may be one, as we are one, I in them
> and you in me, that they may become complete-
> ly one, so that the world may know that you
> have sent me and have loved them even as you
> have loved me. (John 17:22-23)

So where do we go from here? It's interesting. Since our trip to Rome we've discovered that many people in the Protestant world prefer a divided Church. We have personally taken some heat for being willing to meet with the pope (seriously!). But when the most powerful person in the Catholic universe is willing to dialogue about a preferred future in which we actually honor the words and prayer of Jesus, we refuse to be okay with a five-hundred-year-old schism instead. So what will it be? Division or unity?

As a result of seeing up close and personally the historical and current Catholic-Protestant conflict, we cannot "un-see." Seeing creates responsibility, and we now carry a new responsibility in the work of ushering in unity in the Body of Christ for the sake of the Kingdom. We have seen the Kingdom—not just groups and segregated tribes, but we have seen the heart of Jesus for a divided and unkind world, especially within the borders and in the name of religion. The times demand action, demand peacemaking, demand unity. We are never more fully alive than when living the gospel of Jesus Christ in a broken and divided world. This is the space for which the pope and the movement of John 17 have extended an invitation for all.

We have been deeply challenged to initiate invitations to sit around more tables and sit in more spaces where differing voices are safe and can be shared in the spirit of John chapter 17. This is not for someone else to do. It is ours to own and initiate. Since our time with the pope, we have invited new friends, a local imam, a local rabbi, and their wives, over for dinner. We shared a kosher and halal meal, but it was so much more than the food. It was a gathering of friends with a shared desire for unity. We talked about Jesus. We shared our perspectives of our own personal faiths and we committed to stand with one another.

Unity may seem elusive but it is worth everything we have to give to see it happen. We are challenged daily to see everyone as an image bearer of God and to honor our humanity. This is the message for our times and the message to be passed along to future generations. We believe "for such a time as this," with Pope Francis, we must lean in, listen, learn, and practice the ways of love to bring forth a united Kingdom.

God of Surprises

Bishop Peter Smith

It was stunning—and completely unexpected—to attend such a small, personal, and pastoral meeting with Pope Francis. About fifty of us gathered in a meeting room with the pope as he shared from his experience as a pastor.

I like to tell my friends that it is only because of my association with the John 17 Movement and the Evangelical pastors and leaders in it that I was able to meet Pope Francis in this amazing way. Normally, when we Catholic bishops meet the pope it is a very scripted and regimented encounter. I had twice previously met Pope Francis, each time for about thirty seconds at most, allowing me only a quick handshake and a very brief greeting before the papal minders moved me along. But here I was, one of a handful of Catholics with this group of Evangelical leaders, meeting my shepherd—all because of what God is doing through John 17.

I was born and raised in South Africa. Catholics are a minority there, so I related to other Christians and people of other beliefs most of the time. It was effectively training in relational ecumenism. At twenty years of age I had a profound experience of Christ and the Holy Spirit. It changed my life, leading to a great deepening of my relationship with God and of my Catholic faith and practice. It also helped me to relate to other Christians more deeply.

The Lord eventually led me to the United States and to joining the People of Praise community. The People of Praise is a predominantly lay charismatic community. Ecumenism has always been a key element of the community's identity. I have embraced this in my life and my ministry, first as a Catholic priest, and now as a Catholic bishop. And it was Pope Francis who appointed me a bishop, much to my surprise.

Through my association with this community I am currently part of an effort called the Gathering of the Holy Spirit. It is an annual meeting of Catholic and New Charismatic Churches' leaders, in association with the *Centro Pro Unione* in Rome. The goal is to develop deeper fraternal relations and to foster dialogue and greater understanding, both unofficially and officially. At some of these meetings I met and got to know Mike Herron, now one of the key leaders of John 17, as well as Pastor Giovanni Traettino and Matteo Calisi.

Fast forward several years to 2016. Josh Butler, a pastor from Imago Dei Church in Portland, Oregon, was one of the Evangelical leaders who met with Pope Francis in 2016. He returned and shared far and wide his overwhelmingly positive experience of that meeting. Josh then sought to reach out to Catholics. Through the assistance of a mutual friend, I met with both Josh and Mike in Portland. We shared together and prayed together. When praying about whom to invite to the 2017 meeting with Pope Francis, Josh felt led to invite me. And that is how the Holy Spirit worked in so many unexpected and roundabout ways to allow me to be part of the John 17 group in Rome. God is full of surprises.

In the People of Praise we follow a very relational approach to ecumenism. The doctrinal aspects are not ours to deal with, as they are the domain of authorized theologians and Church leaders. But ordinary Catholics are encouraged to pursue a "grassroots ecumenism" or an "ecumenism of life" with other Christians, something both Pope Benedict XVI and Pope Francis have encouraged us to do. We have so much in common as baptized brothers and sisters in Christ even though we may believe and worship differently in some areas. So, we share what we have in common to the degree that we can. And we do so ever mindful of the Catholic Church's principle that to be fully ecumenical we always have to be fully who we are in Christ. In practice this is a relational ecumenism.

Pope Francis wonderfully conveyed the essence of this relational ecumenism to the John 17 group that met with him in 2016. When asked what they could do to build relationships with one another and with Catholics, he responded, "Get a latte or gelato and go for a walk." In my experience, John 17 members have truly sought to put this into action, both on an individual and a group level. Often it has been as simple as having a gathering and introducing our "everyday" friends to our John 17 friends from other Christian and Catholic realms. Food, conversation, and charity often lead to relationship and reconciliation (the movie *Babette's Feast* is a great illustration of this principle in action).

The John 17 Movement embodies this approach and actively promotes it. When we know one another, know one another's faith, and know the workings of God in one another's lives, then being brothers and sisters is not academic any more. We become far more understanding and willing to listen to one another and to love and serve one another. The differences between us remain, and may be painful, but they no longer dominate our relationships. It is love, care, affection, friendship, and the desire to serve and accompany one another that become the predominant locus of our relationships in Christ.

Since the 2017 trip to Rome I have been part of two other events of the John 17 Movement. One was a large gathering of Evangelical pastors and leaders, mainly from the Phoenix area, along with local Catholic leadership. I experienced great openness among the large group of attendees. It was another example of the Holy Spirit working to break down barriers among us and to enable us to encounter one another as brothers and sisters in Christ. I had one particularly moving conversation with an Evangelical church leader and his wife. At the end of the conversation we joined hands and prayed with and for each other. We also agreed to pray for one another in the future, for whatever God may have for us and wherever he may be leading us.

More recently I was able to be present at a two-day planning event for John 17 and to seek direction and input for the future. It was a great experience of prayer, reflection, discussion, and fraternity with all those present. And in an ecumenical twist, we met at a Catholic retreat center. It was another wonderful moment of unity with my Evangelical brothers and sisters. The more we are in Christ and the more he shines in us, the more the desire for unity that comes from Christ arises within us.

There was one moment in the gathering when I was marveling at what God had done and was doing in all of us present, when I had a profound sense of how many lives were being touched and changed through the men and women in that room. I was moved to thank God deeply for all he was doing, so much of it unseen by us. And at the same moment I experienced a great appreciation for how each one of those present had said yes to God and his call and mission for their lives.

What we believe and receive needs to be lived out in our lives, though. God continues to provide me with opportunities to engage in relational ecumenism in the spirit of John 17. One such opportunity was an invitation to give the sermon at two Sunday services for the 500th anniversary of the Reformation at one of the largest Lutheran churches in the area. I shared some of my experiences in ecumenism and the John 17 Movement, noting that we have in common that we are all brothers and sisters in Christ and are called to treat one another as such.

Another opportunity was an invitation to share the reflection for evensong at a local Anglican church during Advent. The pastor is a young married man who has a deep desire for greater unity among Christians. Afterward I was blessed to have good conversations with some of the attendees regarding scripture. Only then did they realize I was a

Catholic bishop. It was a great moment for all of us to realize in a very practical way our common bond in Christ.

As the John 17 Movement develops and grows I am looking forward to seeing what God does in having us not only embody the spirit of ecumenism in our own lives and ministries, including our own churches, but also in working together. The witness of different Christians working side by side is a powerful answer to the scandal of divisions among us.

May the prayer of Jesus for his disciples and us to grow in unity be answered more and more in the witness of our lives and our faith. And may our lives help make Christ shine more and more fully in his creation until all are united in him.

Children of One Father

Peter Petrov

I was a little kid growing up in a communist country when I first faced the division between the capitalist world and us. It was always "them" and "us." Them, who had no faces, them, who had no dreams—or at least their dreams were not good for us. They were strangers and we, the communists, had nothing in common with them and we did not want to. In other words, they were the enemy.

Time passed and democracy came to my country, Bulgaria. Communism was gone. Christianity, which had been in our lands for ages before, was now back. With its return came some old questions, although they were new for me: three churches, three different denominations, three distinct traditions. The same Father's children, who did not accept their brotherhood. I found myself in that old time of division, where different belief systems argue about which one is more right, and in the meantime the people suffer.

I read the Bible with the eyes and consciousness of a child, and I did not understand why they would not see what I saw inside this book. It was so clearly written, in my opinion. Later I realized that their disputes were really important for them, and their differences were a matter of serious debate, beside which my questions about the love between God and us looked naïve and childish.

Geopolitical and cultural peculiarities, which in fact are so deeply connected with the emotions of each individual and society, made unity among the believers hard and according to some, even impossible. Every single community lives in its own lake, its own kingdom. Every individual experiences some kind of identity crisis and needs an added value that his group gives him. Each Christian community proclaims the Kingdom of Heaven, but doesn't look towards the neighboring lake.

One day while I was traveling to Rome with my friend Joseph Tosini I closed my eyes and looked at these lakes in a new way. No matter how hard we try to connect those lakes into one, we eventually get a bigger one, but still a lake. Then I realized that Christianity is a river. There is no way we could ever be a family if everyone lived in his own bubble, or his own lake. We needed a river, springing from the top of the mountain, providing living water.

People naturally form social groups; they like doing that. We can see it in every club, whether it's a sports club, a political club, or a religious one. Even monkeys do it, but is that what really should have happened to Christianity? Can representatives of the distinct lakes meet on neutral territory and communicate? Is that enough? Or should we approach each other the way Jesus did when he showed us the example of washing each other's feet?

On this trip to Rome we got to meet Pope Francis. Joseph, as a co-founder and leader of the John 17 Movement, and I, who came across all this completely accidentally and not deservedly, and a small group of pastors. This meeting with the head of the Roman Catholic Church was a surprise to me. I saw in his face a humble and wise man with a sense of humor. The ease with which he communicated with our group and his attitude toward the unity of the Church made me feel understood. I was no longer alone in my naïve visions that we can be together. Being surrounded by people who see the world with the same eyes gave me a piece of heaven. It was a real family. Love was the cornerstone of our conversation and of the renewal of relationships. Through a true and deep love for Christ, we could restore our broken relationships and create this living river. This is what I understood that day; it changed my life forever.

Some people would see this as unification, but unification would happen if we just create a big still lake, with no connection with God and his prophetic spark. The river is different, all along its different stages. It washes us naturally through its flow. This is not unification of institutions and religious structures, because the Church of Christ has always been and will always be one in actuality. We are the ones who have separated it and institutionalized it. This is a return to our Father. It is to sit at the table together and forget about our human limitations and different perceptions. The same way there is unity in diversity and integrated complexity in the universe, so we in the Body of Christ are one by love, but not losing our uniqueness.

We pray for the Kingdom of God to come, but what about the three churches in Bulgaria? I find that some people are confused, because they naturally want to respond to the call for unity—as Christ clearly called us to do in John chapter 17—but they are afraid. Sometimes they have to face a complicated choice about whom they should serve. In situations like this, I remember how the Pharisees tried to trap Jesus, asking him about a coin that depicted the Roman emperor. His answer was really right: we need to give to God what belongs to God (cf. Matthew 22:21).

Sometimes we serve our religious community, our country, or our family. But when they come into contradiction, when something stops us from reaching out to the rest of the people through love, or when something is hindering us from following the prayer of Christ in chapter 17 of John's Gospel, we should ask ourselves a question. What is more important: Jesus Christ or our theology, our culture, and our dogmas?

Pope Francis talked about how unity starts with just eating one ice cream together and getting to know each other, leaving theology to the side. How lovely it would be to leave aside the arguments we've had for ages and agree that we don't know everything, that we are children of the same Father, brothers and sisters. And the things we do know about, we just need to accomplish. Unfortunately we have chosen the easier path: to argue about the things we don't know, to pretend we understand it all, and to judge the rest according to our own understanding. As for the clear and obvious things—love and faith—we choose to hide from and avoid them. Spending months of research on the Internet about someone, collecting opinions about him or her, doesn't mean anything compared with taking a simple step toward this individual. To go to him, to hear her, to hug him, even metaphorically speaking. I saw the result of this with my own eyes, and I believe that I have touched a part of God's Kingdom this way.

The Father's Heart

Brian and Gina Kruckenberg

Growing Up Outside the Church (Brian)

While it might appear that my John 17 journey began two years ago when I first met Joseph Tosini, my journey actually has roots much further back than I could ever have imagined.

I did not grow up in a Christian home. I like to say that I grew up "around" church, but not in it. It isn't as if I never heard the gospel of Jesus, but it was only a few times in my early childhood. By God's grace and in his providence, when I was a senior in high school my art teacher shared the gospel with me and some of my friends. We were curious, and we asked him if he would lead us in a Bible study. We chose the one of two books every non-Christian knows: we asked him to take us through Revelation! And he did it! (Although I'm sure he was praying for us to say Genesis.) Our study group of four turned into about forty by the end of the year, and I was baptized in a small country church in Kansas when I was eighteen. A few months later, though, I packed up and went to college several hours away with no Christian foundation and no Christian friends.

Fast-forward about eight years: I had finished my undergraduate, graduate, and law degrees. I was newly married and landed a job at a large law firm in downtown Kansas City, Missouri. Life was good, but I was miserable because I was running from Jesus. Again, by the grace of God, there was another new attorney at the firm who kept inviting me to church. I started by just saying, "no," then, "maybe," then finally, "yes," but with no intention of actually showing up. But once I finally did show up, on January 30, 2000, God got me! I quit running from him and immediately began to discover this God I had been avoiding most of my life.

I dove into serving the church, and I began to consume the Bible like I would a law book. I devoured it and attended every Bible study possible. Eventually I left the full-time practice of law. Now, eighteen years after that encounter with God, I serve as the lead pastor of New City Church in downtown Phoenix, which my wife and I started with a few friends in 2011. God has been so good to us.

Growing Up Catholic (Gina)

Much like Brian, I had no idea where my John 17 journey started until I reflected on it over the past two years. I was raised as a Catholic. My Catholic experience was probably pretty typical. I went to Mass regularly as a child and was confirmed after taking classes in the Confraternity of Christian Doctrine (CCD, or Sunday School). I was taught that Jesus died for my sins and that I should pray regularly. Yet, for whatever reason, my faith never seemed that personal to me. I remember wanting to be involved in church, but I never knew exactly how to do that. Still, I felt that my faith was an important part of my life.

As Brian described, a few months after we were married, we finally found a church where God seemed to speak to us. There were lots of young people from all over the world (it was near a university with many international students) and we were immediately involved in small groups and Bible studies. Of course, as we got to know more people, we told them our stories and how we ended up at that church. Part of my story was my Catholic background.

This is perhaps where my John 17 journey began, because I soon learned that my Catholic upbringing was something that I had to "overcome." I don't know what exactly it was, but when I told people that I was raised Catholic I was treated like I had to unlearn or forget much of what I had been taught. I found this a little strange and, to be honest, hurtful, because while I knew I had much to grow in, I also knew that my Catholic upbringing had taught me some valuable things about God. I knew that Jesus is God's Son and I knew that Jesus paid the price for my sins. Never did I feel like I didn't understand that. Like many, I didn't have a fully formed theology of salvation, but certainly I knew that Jesus saves.

As Brian and I continued on our faith journey together, my experience in other churches was similar. People I met at church often called themselves ex-Catholics. This was confusing to me as I always thought of myself as a Christian, even as a Catholic. I went to a Catholic church growing up, and I was a Christian. I wondered why the two couldn't go together. Thankfully, I would eventually discover that they could!

Church and the Art of Subtle Disunity (Brian)

The funny thing about getting deeply involved in church is that you are quickly taught, either directly or by osmosis, that your church is different from other churches—and by different, I really mean better. The other churches are good, but they don't disciple people like we do. The other churches are great, but their teaching isn't as deep as ours. Yes, God is using other churches, but are they as "Spirit-filled" as ours? In other words, you quickly learn to think that your "little c" church is *the* Church! It is incredible how quickly it happened to me, and I didn't have any church loyalties at all before I was twenty-six years old. I didn't know a Baptist from a Methodist from a Presbyterian (or even what that was), and I didn't care. But within a year at a particular church, I found myself judging the ministry of others. In part I was taught to do this and in part it was just my legalistic "sibling" heart, not liking how my other brothers and sisters did things.

After two years at the first church we attended (which did teach me so many wonderful things about Jesus and the power of the Holy Spirit), my wife and I transitioned to a different church that was much closer to home. We had been driving about forty-five miles each way to our first church, and with my wife expecting our first child, we knew we needed to be closer to home to have the community we really desired. We were also sharing our faith with our friends and wanted them to be able to come with us to church. So we found a church close by and started getting involved just like before: serving, small groups, and Bible studies. It was great.

But, again, it wasn't long before we started feeling the same things. Our new church wasn't as charismatic as our first church and some in our new church questioned many charismatic practices. Some of it was in good faith and biblically based, but much of it was simply divisive. And again, there was this feeling that our church was different from others, that is, we were "more biblical." We learned there are right and wrong ways to "do church." These differences could be found in just about anything: teaching, worship, programming, church leadership structure, etc. Much like siblings, churches can argue over just about anything. It's uncanny.

None of these differences compared to the doubts and questions surrounding the Catholic Church. I had had some exposure to Catholicism since the small town where I went to high school had a massive Catholic church, and for the most part anyone I knew who went to church attended there. I also had an uncle on my father's side of the family who was a practicing Catholic, and during the summer when we were at the lake, he would drive his boat across the lake to attend Mass every Sunday without fail.

But, again, somewhere along the way, I learned that Catholics aren't Christians. They "pray to Mary," have a religious hierarchy, and believe that works, not grace, save you. So I put Catholics in the non-Christian category and didn't give it much thought.

A John 17 Revelation (Brian)

So, this is where our journey intersects with the John 17 Movement. I was introduced to Joseph Tosini in the spring of 2016 and was told that he was going to Rome that summer to meet with Pope Francis. I was told I might be invited along. *Sure,* I thought. *Going to meet the pope. Right.* Well, I met with Joseph. Just a few months later I was on a plane with other pastors on a pilgrimage to the Vatican to sit down with Pope Francis and talk about Church unity and our oneness in Christ.

It is interesting how the Lord works, because the most impactful moment for me on that first trip happened before I ever met Pope Francis. It was the night before we were to visit the pope and we had just enjoyed a meal with pastors from around the world. Joseph shared a story from his life, reflecting on a conversation that he and his brother had had at his mother's memorial service. As they were talking, one turned to the other and said, "You know, all Mom ever wanted was for us to be together." A simple truth, yet powerful because it is so deeply true! I immediately thought of my mother and my two brothers. I know that the one thing my mom wants more than anything is for her sons to love each other. We lost our father in 2001, and she often says that she knows Dad would want us to be together. Not in the same city, mind you, but *together.* To be *one.*

Joseph continued by relating his mother's heart to our Father's heart. That we might be one! That we would not have a sibling's heart toward each other (I can't help but think of the prodigal son and his elder brother), but that we would love each other as the Father loves his Son.

> I ask not only on behalf of these, but also on behalf of those who will believe in me through their word, that *they may all be one. As you, Father, are in me and I am in you, may they also be in us*, so that the world may believe that you have sent me. (John 17:20-21, emphasis added)

That was it! Too often I have seen others from my sibling's heart. Finding fault. Finding ways we disagree. All along God has wanted me to have *his* heart for others, a heart of love and sacrifice. That is the Father's heart and from that heart people can see the truth about Jesus. Our love for each other is not only essential for our Christian discipleship, but also an imperative for Christian evangelism. How could I ignore this biblical truth? It makes complete sense. When people love each other, it is attractive. We want to be with people who love each other. When people fight and bicker, it is off-putting. One car ride with siblings fighting over one square inch of the backseat tells a person that. Love, as someone once said, is the true apologetic.

Healing Old Wounds (Gina)

The year after Brian met with Pope Francis, I got to go on the return trip along with him and others. One of the driving principles of the John 17 Movement is that "unity starts at the feet and not at the head," so as part of our trip in Rome, we washed the feet of strangers whom we had just met. This act of service did just what it was supposed to do: humble us. As Jesus modeled for us, those who want to be great in the Kingdom of God must serve others. Taking Jesus seriously in his command by doing this simple but profound act allowed me to see just how many of our "differences" really do not amount to much when we serve the other. When you actually practice what Jesus taught, it becomes clear why Jesus wanted us to serve each other as a way to get to know each other. Serving the other means that you honor and respect them simply for who they are: a person made in the image of God. Serving others shows that we all need each other in order to truly know God and his heart for all people.

The trip proved to be therapeutic and healing for me. While in Rome, I was able to meet with many Protestants and Catholics and listen to their stories. I was struck by how everyone had Jesus at the center. Yes, people worshiped differently, and people definitely held different beliefs about certain Christian practices, but at the core was the understanding that Jesus is Lord and he alone saves.

As I heard from Catholics and got to meet so many wonderful people, God began to show me that my Catholic upbringing was not something that I had to "work through," be ashamed of, or forget. For the first time in my life, I began to *embrace* what I had learned in the Catholic Church and saw how what I had learned over the past eighteen years in the Protestant/Evangelical Church worked together with my early faith. It says in the Bible that it is for freedom that we have been set free. That seems almost redundant, but during my trip to Rome this powerful truth hit me like never before. I suddenly had a freedom in my faith that I hadn't previously experienced. It feels so good to be free, knowing that God used all aspects of my life and faith journey to make me the person I am today.

The Church United (Together)

The time we actually spent with Pope Francis was a tremendous blessing. Perhaps one of the biggest and most important revelations we had was that the movement of unity we are experiencing isn't about the pope. It is about what Jesus prayed for and what the Holy Spirit is doing. Our time with Pope Francis just underscored that. When we gathered together, we sang hymns and prayed for one another. Then we simply talked. While we did ask Pope Francis questions, our time with him was much more a dialogue than him teaching or preaching. We were struck by his humility and his grace. In his answers to various questions, he would often quote scripture and give his thoughts on what the scripture taught about things like leadership, worship, and discipling children. At the end of his answers, he often closed with the words, "These are my thoughts, but I am just a man. You should read the text and pray and seek answers from God himself."

During our conversation, the pope took the time to answer every question asked of him, and then he graciously visited with each of us, allowing us to take a photo with him to remember this special time. Here was one of the most powerful men in the world, and he gave us extra time and did so willingly! It was clear that Pope Francis has an earnest desire to see the Church unite around the name of Jesus. He was not trying to convince us to become Catholic; on the contrary, he told us that we should all stay where we are called and live out the ministry of reconciliation in our own contexts. He encouraged us, as leaders in the Church, to have a "ministry of the ears," making it a point to listen to others as a way to find unity. He said that if we cannot take the time to listen, then we cannot love as God calls us to love.

Where our John 17 journey will go from here we cannot really know. What we do know is that we have had our eyes opened to the vastness of the Kingdom of God. We have learned that Jesus is so much bigger than we often think, because we tend to limit the ways of Jesus to our ways. We know that if we are to honor the prayer of our Savior, we must work toward unity, because in the unity of the Body, people will know that God sent his Son Jesus into the world. Making Jesus known to the world is essential to our mission. Therefore, working for unity in the Church is a non-negotiable essential for every Christian.

God Is Love

Pat Markey

As I grew up in my solidly practicing Catholic family, I
became aware of seemingly irreconcilable divisions in the
world around me. As a teenager I remember being scandal-
ized during my visit to a Catholic parish on the opposite
side of town. While the parish I belonged to was large, thriv-
ing, and somewhat affluent, this church was in a very poor
neighborhood, and from my perspective, quite rundown. I
also could not help but notice that, as opposed to where I
lived, the majority of the people in the neighborhood were
of a darker complexion. To me it was a scandal: how could it
be that after the work of Martin Luther King, Jr., there was
still such racial and social inequality? Even worse, how could
it exist in the Church, which was supposed to offer a new
Christian view of society?

My way of confronting this problem was rejection. I
was fifteen and decided to reject the injustices of the world
by focusing exclusively on sports and to reject the hypocrisy
of the Church by walking away from it altogether. This was
an effective approach until my sister invited me to join some
friends of hers in a group called the "Focolare" for a weekend
at a Texas dude ranch.

Although my sister and her friends had been involved
with this group for years, I never bothered to find out what
it was or what they did. She was older than me so that approach seemed to make sense. I arrived late Friday night
after a track meet. The people I met were very nice and

welcoming; it helped that I knew some of them from the neighborhood. Imagine my surprise Saturday morning when I walked into a small meeting hall and learned that it was a retreat on the gospel call to love our neighbor! While I should have been angry for being duped, I was actually quite intrigued. I remember in that opening session the presenter explained that the weekend would not just be studying and praying (although there would be that); more than anything else it would be an experience of living, of putting into practice what was said and understood.

I still have a hard time explaining what happened a few hours later in that same small hall. What I can say is I had an encounter that changed my life forever. I was listening intently to what others said and I remember that it must have involved Paul's First Letter to the Corinthians, that beautiful ode to love, "Love is patient; love is kind . . ." (1 Corinthians 13:4ff). Suddenly I understood. But it was more than an understanding: it was an encounter. I met someone who told me to replace the word "love" with "God." I did so, and like being hit by lightning I understood that God is love. All of a sudden everything made sense to me. It is all about love. What we have to do is love. The problems, divisions, and scandals I see, even in the Church, stem from a lack of love. Now that I had met Love, I understood I had a responsibility. I could no longer run away from or reject what was happening around me. I had to love.

Luckily, my new friends from the Focolare had an approach to putting love into practice. They would take a sentence from scripture and live it in their day-to-day lives. Not just read it, study it, or pray it, but actually live it. When they come together, they tell each other what happened as a result. It worked! Living scripture gave me a way to love continually. Although I really was not that good at it, this approach to life changed everything for me. In time I came to understand that at the core of the gospel message is Jesus' last will and testament, his prayer to the Father in John chapter 17. In fact, this is what Chiara Lubich, the Focolare founder, and her followers dedicated all their lives and efforts toward: unity. I too made unity, the fulfillment of Jesus' prayer, the center and goal of my life. I was never very religious, and I'm still not, but I do believe that love is the only remedy to the world's ills and that love ultimately leads to unity.

One particularly strong experience happened in the summer of 1982. I went on a Focolare summer retreat called a Mariapolis. These events involve people from all walks of life and take place all over the world. That year, Chiara had prepared a theme on unity that we focused on and tried to live during that week together. She proposed what she called the "Art of Loving." To be a builder of unity we would have to live like Jesus. How did Jesus live? First, he considered everyone a candidate for unity. No one was excluded, no one. We should do likewise with every person that crosses our path. The question of who our neighbor is, she said, is very simple: it is the person next to us in the present moment. And the way to love that person? By serving them, just as Jesus washed the feet of his apostles. Then, she continued, we need to make ourselves one with that neighbor. His or her concerns should genuinely be our own. Eventually the person responds and then love becomes mutual. If we are both ready to give our lives as Jesus did, then, as he promised in Matthew 18:20, he will be in our midst and he will be the one to bring about unity. "For where two or three are gathered in my name, I am there among them." His name is who he is: love. He is present among us in a real, if unseen, way. We too become a living presence of Jesus in the world.

I tried to live as a builder of unity during that summer and I can honestly say that I had a strong and lasting experience of Jesus' presence, of paradise on earth. For the first time I understood what it means to be one with others because of Jesus' presence among us. It was during that time that he called me to follow him in a deeper, more serious way.

In time I would dedicate my entire life to Jesus and living for unity. He asked me to do so in the Focolare, helping others to understand and work for unity. "Focolare" is a nickname that signifies the warmth of fire and light—a *focolare* is a hearth in old Italian kitchens. The movement's official name is the Work of Mary. The Focolare's role is to be like Mary the Mother of Jesus, of God. Of Mary's life we know very little. What we do know is that she did God's will and gave Jesus to the world. This is the path I have tried, sometimes with success and sometimes without, to follow. Without my looking for anything, it has led me on a wonderfully exciting adventure that I never could have imagined. I have been around the world, with kings and presidents and religious leaders of all kinds. I have had the honor of being with the poor, the dying, AIDs victims in New York and throughout Africa, refugees, orphans, and the undocumented in faraway countries and close at home in the United States. I worked on Wall Street and as a publisher, raised money and ran grant programs for the Catholic Church, and now I assist finance and accounting professionals who work for the Church.

Most readers of this book will never have heard of the Focolare. In a way, that gives me comfort, because the work of unity should always point to Jesus and the life of the Trinity, in which he has invited us to participate. The vehicle that brings us there is not as important.

Unfortunately, disunity can be found everywhere, and like a soothing, countering presence working in the background, that is where the Focolare tries to be. Nevertheless, I must confess that after growing up in Texas, the last place I imagined unity would reach would be between Catholics and Evangelicals. I personally experienced such animosity, and probably added to it, that I had concluded that perhaps Catholics and Evangelicals could never come together in a real, constructive, and loving way. Individually, yes, I have good friends and family members who are Evangelical, but as groups I just could not see it.

Through simple circumstances and an act of love—a relationship—I came to know Joseph and Mary Tosini and heard their vision for John 17. They told me that they were preparing to take a group of Evangelical, Protestant, and Catholic leaders to see Pope Francis. I could hardly believe my ears! When they returned from that first meeting I could see that something really exceptional had happened. It was more than just the excitement of meeting the pope. Something had occurred among those who made the trip. They experienced Jesus' loving, uniting presence among them. They lived an experience of unity and it changed everything.

Now our little Focolare group in Phoenix is journeying with the growing John 17 group. I have no doubt that God has a divine plan and that he is using us all as instruments to bring the vitally important message of unity, of John 17, to many, many people. Like I said, this journey of unity has led me to many amazing places, but seeing unity among Evangelicals, Catholics, and Protestants is the most beautiful yet!

Seeds of Love

Michael Rudzena

I live in New York City. When our family bought a one-way ticket and arrived seven years ago in a Lower Manhattan neighborhood called Tribeca, we were eager. Eager to settle our family of four into a new city, to meet people and build friendships, to start a church from scratch in a neighborhood with no church buildings.

But we soon experienced the delightfully complicated challenge of New York: her diversity. Diversity of classes, diversity of races, diversity of religions, diversity of politics, diversity of sexuality.

Our experience of faith up to that point was thoroughly Evangelical, and it came with a certain posture toward the outsider. It was laced with an addictive tendency toward like-mindedness and a vague suspicion of difference. Most of the churches we had experienced looked, thought, and acted like us: mostly white, mostly conservative, mostly straight, mostly middle- to upper-middle class. But now we were immersed in a neighborhood and network of friendships where this small security of similarity was no longer available. We were presented not simply with the idea of difference, but its lived experience.

In the face of such difference, the basic mode of operation I had been taught in my Evangelical experience was to defend and convert. Sure, it was meant to be done in a winsome and intelligent way, but in the end my job was to help the outsiders become insiders. To translate the faith. To invite people into faith commitments. To address the hardest questions head on. It was the ministry of the Word.

Up to that point, most of my Evangelical friends considered Catholics to be such outsiders. When talking about the state of Christianity in Manhattan, for instance, we would ignore the significant Catholic presence and cite the scarce 3% of residents who called themselves Evangelical. Many of these friends, like my own family of origin, had left their loose association with the Catholic Church to become "true Christians" through the ministry of their Evangelical church. For us, secular New Yorkers weren't the only objects of our mission; Catholics were too. Then things became complicated.

The secular New Yorkers were so good at seeing our Evangelical blind spots and hypocrisies. They were often people of deep intelligence, integrity, and openness. One observation I consistently heard was about the divided state of the Christian Church. To most of my neighbors, Catholics and Evangelicals were in the same camp. Why didn't or couldn't we get along? If this "good news" I was talking about was so good, why couldn't it address the simple "insider" challenges of our own religion?

Rather than pridefully dismissing these critiques and doubling down on my enlightened insider perspective, I wrestled with these questions and searched for answers. I went back to the Bible with new questions and new eyes. What I found was not new content, but new resonance.

For example, I started to wrestle with the prayer of Jesus in John chapter 17. What did Jesus mean when he prayed that we would become one just as the Trinity is one? Why did Jesus connect our unity as insiders with the legitimacy of Jesus in the eyes of outsiders? This prayer resonated in a brand-new way, and it forced me to begin rethinking my relationship with my Catholic brothers and sisters.

After several years of grappling with this idea, I finally met a man named Joseph Tosini. I was told he was a bridge builder—someone with deep Evangelical roots as well as thick

Catholic ties. I showed up to a meeting on Long Island and heard his testimony. He described a remarkable movement of relationships emerging in Phoenix and said they were beginning to identify the work as the John 17 Movement.

One evening at the Church of St. Paul the Apostle near Columbus Circle, I participated in a gathering of prayer and worship for Catholics and Evangelicals. Pope Francis had given Joseph a letter to read at the gathering encouraging the effort of John 17. We also heard the testimony of Giovanni, a man who was walking in reconciliation with Pope Francis himself and leading the way of Evangelical and Catholic bridge building in Italy. I was moved.

In 2016, shortly after Pope Francis's visit to New York the previous fall, I was invited to join a small John 17 delegation to the Vatican to meet with the leader of the largest Christian denomination in the world. I had no idea what to expect. I was prepared for the extreme formality of official ecumenical dialogue, but what I actually experienced changed my life.

The meeting lasted roughly two hours. Pope Francis set the relational tone early on by suggesting that we share our hearts with one another as sisters and brothers. He immediately told us that when people are martyred in our time, they aren't asked if they are Catholic or Evangelical, they are asked if they are Christians. How is it that our enemies see our essential unity, but we can't?

I had the opportunity to ask Pope Francis a personal question. I asked him to put himself in my shoes. If he were a young leader in New York at this moment in history, what would he prioritize? His answer has shaped the core of my ministry over the past three years.

He replied, "What I am about to tell you may sound strange, because it is a minister's job to proclaim a message. We have the ministry of the Word. My advice to you is this: Listen to the people. Prioritize the 'ministry of the ear.' The Word in the heart of a person is like a small seed that the Lord will grow."

These words touched my spirit. I came to New York and to my Catholic friends ready to proclaim, to sow seeds. But was I really open to listening? Was my heart open to having the seed of another's words planted in my heart to help me grow and change?

From that point on, my posture toward my own congregation, my Catholic friends, and my neighborhood at large was transformed. No longer did I see my relationship to the city and my friends as a one-sided negotiation. Rather, I had new eyes to appreciate the two-way relationship with an emphasis on listening. This is, after all, the nature of love: a genuine openness to the other. I have begun to have eyes to see God's love and presence at work in my Catholic brothers and sisters in ways I never thought possible. I've begun to expect God to be at work in my neighbor as I listen to their lives and hopes and fears. I see my solidarity with them in a new light and am more committed than ever to building bridges rather than reinforcing walls.

This doesn't mean we must ignore or gloss over difference. It simply means we gain eyes to see, learn, listen, and appreciate the beauty and dignity of our neighbor. It simply means living out Jesus' command to love our neighbor as ourselves. And in this love, we experience a fresh communion: a foretaste of the fulfillment of Jesus' prayer in John chapter 17.

A Change of Heart

Ryan Nunez

I have been in church all my life. When I was born, I was literally brought home from the hospital to the church. Well, technically, our home was the parsonage at the front of the church, but it's pretty close. You see, my dad was an associate pastor at a Baptist church, as was his father before him. I grew up in very traditional Baptist churches and I attended private Christian schools until the fifth grade.

Although my world revolved around church, my view of Christianity was very small. There were never any overt criticisms that I can remember, but I picked up things here and there—passing comments about another denomination, prayer requests for people who got caught up in "unbiblical" churches. The only things I knew about other Christians were what people told me; I didn't personally know anyone outside my association of churches. No one would actually come out and say it, but I determined pretty quickly that we were the ones who were doing Christianity right and everyone else was doing it wrong. I felt so fortunate that I was born into this particular church tradition and not one of the others.

That all began to change as I entered high school and college. I began developing real friendships with other Christians who didn't attend my church. I was so shocked when we would talk about Jesus—it was like we were talking about the same person! And what was even crazier was that we actually believed the same things about salvation and grace. In fact, we didn't have any conflicts in our beliefs. Now, full disclosure, we didn't discuss eschatology, predestination, or gifts of the Spirit. And why would we? We were just friends talking about our relationship with Jesus. Looking back, I now see how important that distinction was. Our bond grew by what we agreed on, not where we disagreed.

Barriers were breaking down and I was beginning to find out how big the Church actually was. But there was still a huge divide that I had not crossed, the Protestant-Catholic line. I held so many preconceived beliefs about Catholics: their mysterious rituals, praying to saints, and the whole "Mary thing"—I just couldn't reconcile all this with Protestant theology. And then I had one of the most eye-opening lunches of my life.

I was new to being a lead pastor. It was never part of my plan to lead a church. I was going to be a scientist. No really, I was! Lots of college and a Ph.D. had me on a trajectory towards a research role in a lab or university, but God had other plans. I found myself in a small church plant helping my former youth pastor get launched, and then the church took off. God was doing something big in this work. Within a few years I was in full-time pastoral ministry in this fast-growing mega church in the West Valley of Phoenix. Then tragedy struck. A health crisis and the devastating loss of our founding pastor placed me in the role of pastoring this church. I was out of my league and reaching out to any pastor for guidance and support as we navigated this incredibly difficult season as a church and as I navigated the loss personally. I had many pastors come and sit with me during this season and offer much-needed advice, but it was my lunch with Gary Kinnaman that sparked something new in me.

Over great Mexican food, Gary told me about an incredible encounter he'd recently had. A former member of his church had converted to Catholicism and invited him to a dinner at his home with the local bishop. To be honest, I wasn't tracking the story all that well at first because I was hung up on the fact that he lost one of his members to the Catholic Church. Sure, I was struggling, but maybe it was him that really needed the help. Eventually, I got out of my judgmental mindset and re-engaged with his actual story. He told me about the friendship that had sparked over dinner and how they wrapped up the evening by reading John chapter 17 and praying together. It was a real Holy Spirit moment.

I cannot explain why this impacted me so much, but it did. Gary really didn't go into detail, but I could tell by the way he was talking and by the language he used—the language of unity—that something incredible had happened that night. Something happened in me too. Gary simply asked at the end of our conversation if pursuing unity between Catholics and Protestants was something I would like to be involved in. They had started John 17, a group that primarily met just for prayer. I simply responded, "yes." I can only point to the Holy Spirit as the source of that response because I typically do not commit to things easily.

I couldn't get this brief encounter out of my mind, and when I went back to the office, I pulled out my Bible and reflected on the passage. If unity among Christians is the heart of Jesus, it needs to be my heart too. I began to feel those same feelings I felt so many years ago when "the Church" grew beyond the boundaries of my small denomination.

Was God asking me to stretch my boundaries of the Church again?

But there were so many things we didn't agree on. I had studied the Reformation, and we were on the right side. Indulgences, primacy of scripture, faith alone, grace alone—we are not compatible. But I felt God urging me to dig a little deeper. The Holy Spirit was compelling me to investigate a little more about what had happened in the five hundred years since the Reformation.

I dove in and began reading the documents of Vatican Council II. I read all I could find on Pope Francis. Many of the assumptions I believed about the Catholic Church were simply not true. What I have realized is that most Protestants' view of the Catholic Church is based on the time of the Reformation. The assumption is that nothing has changed since that point in time. How mistaken I was on that account! I am sure there are many reading right now who want the details, who want me to lay out the theology and work through these differences. But I'm not going to do that. That's for another place and probably another author. You see, although theology is important and necessary, it was not the game changer for me. The biggest changes happened in my heart.

I now felt a burden to pursue unity, not just in Catholic and Protestant relations, but also in every area of my life—with the pastor down the street and with the member of my church who left. I didn't have a full-blown plan or strategy. I didn't even have a comprehensive way to think about it, other than Jesus' prayer of unity for his disciples and me (one of "those who will believe in me through their word," John 17:20).

Clarity came in a very unexpected way, although I should have seen it coming, based on my previous experiences. Somehow, I knew that the path forward would be relational. Up to this point, that was the avenue God used to open my eyes to the size and scope of his Kingdom: relationships in high school and college; hearing from a friend about a friendship he was developing with Catholic leaders. I had a sense that the Holy Spirit would provide opportunities for more relationships to guide me forward, but I would never in a million years have guessed what form that relational encounter would take.

My phone vibrated as I was sitting in a conference. As I walked out of the meeting, I listened to a voicemail from Gary. I should have kept it, but it has long since been deleted. It said something to the effect of, "Hey Ryan, if you are still serious about all this John 17 stuff, we have a group going to Rome to meet with Pope Francis. Let me know if you want to come."

Seriously? I thought. *This has to be a joke, or even worse, a mistake. Maybe he thought he was calling someone else and acci-*

dentally dialed my number. I mean, I am brand new to this effort. God is currently *working on me in this area.* But before the organizers could realize that they invited the wrong guy, I accepted, purchased a ticket, and made my way to Rome. God was obviously up to something and I was looking forward to having a front row seat to the action.

To be honest, my expectations for the actual meeting were quite low. Expect the worst and then hope for a surprise—this strategy had served me well throughout my teen years and I believed it would be the best approach to such an unbelievable invitation. *It will be a quick audience,* I told myself. *Formal. Walk in, sit down, and listen to a short address. The address will be rather generic, lacking any specific language that would either create a sense of unity or cause any disagreement. At the end of the day it will be a really cool experience and a story I will tell my kids for years: the day their dad was in the same room as the pope.*

To say my expectations were exceeded would be a gross understatement. Every expectation I had about the pope was shattered as he quietly walked into the room unannounced, unaccompanied, and unpretentious. We didn't start with formalities. We started by singing a song together and praying together. We then asked questions and had a discussion. Not a deeply theological discussion, but one about our Savior Jesus. To put it in a word, it was relational.

The tone was relational. The language was relational. In fact, I believe it went even deeper than that—it was friendly.

We talked about a lot of things during that two-hour meeting. But what stuck with me was what God had already begun working on in my life. That's how the Holy Spirit works. God is all knowing and all-powerful. My life is not just a series of random events and encounters. I believe God is guiding and directing me. His knowledge has no bounds. He began his work in me in very small ways as I developed friendships in high school. He developed his work further through the planting of a church targeted toward people from all different backgrounds and life stages, and began to sharpen and focus it through my transition in leadership. He clarified and put language to his work in this meeting with Pope Francis and many other fellow brothers and sisters in Christ. I walked out with clarity on how I would pursue unity in my life, my church, my local community, and the Church at large.

Two phrases shared by Pope Francis in the meeting have stayed with me. The first phrase is: "Unity is not uniformity." The goal of unity is not for everyone to be the same. I have preached on the Body of Christ countless times over the years, but my application and my view have always been through the lens of the local church. The local church is my life, and I believe it is the hope of the world. Each person in a local body has a role to play to serve each other and function in a healthy way to do the work of Christ. However, I had not viewed this idea through the lens of the entire Church. The worldwide Church is the Body of Christ. Each local church also has a role to play and function to perform for the benefit and health of the entire body. There are hands, feet, heart, lungs, and legs. Each part is important, and each part is different and unique. There is unity in the body as a whole, but the parts are not uniform. So the interpretation is not local church vs. universal Church. It is both. The local church is a body made up of many parts and the global Church is a body made up of many parts. Jesus is the head of both at the same time. In fact, it is Jesus who brings the unity. It is Jesus who identifies us as part of the same body. If you don't recognize Jesus as the head, we are not part of the same body. But if you do, we should be in unity.

The second phrase is: "Unity starts with friendship." This resonated with me because it has been my experience. I hadn't seen the pattern until then, but every step I had taken toward unity up to that point in my life involved conversations with people. Friendships developed over our sharing life experiences and finding common ground. Like I said before, theology is important. I have some deep theological convictions that I don't dismiss casually or haphazardly. But theological discussions tend to divide. If we start with division, we end up with division. But if we start with friendship, we build towards unity. Pope Francis said in the meeting that he believes that all theologians, both Catholic and Protestant, will come into complete agreement—the day after Jesus returns. When we start with friendship, we build a solid relational foundation that can stand up to the difficulties of theological disagreement. Unity is developed during walks and meals, not in debates and lectures.

I came back from Rome excited about what God was doing in the area of unity. We have a unique window of opportunity with what God started in the hearts of a few pastors and a pope who desire the same thing. *But how do we keep momentum going?* I wondered. *How do I get my local church involved? Do they even want to be involved? Am I going to lose my job or a bunch of church members over my meeting with the pope?*

I pastor a very loving and outward-focused church. The vast majority of our church body was previously unchurched or living outside a relationship with Jesus Christ before they came to Palm Valley Church. However, I know the historical biases. I know that pastors in my denomination in the past (and even some in the present) identify the pope with the antichrist, and the Catholic Church with the Babylon imagery in the Book of Revelation. If these thoughts and beliefs were in my church, while they would be a small minority, they could cause some major issues.

How much of the story do I tell? How do I frame it? God, give me the words.

The Holy Spirit guided my words that Sunday to be sure. I talked about my meeting with Pope Francis not as a meeting of Protestant-Catholic relations, not as a meeting of institutions and organizations, but as a meeting of Church leaders who really believe that Jesus wants his Church to be unified. We know this because he prayed for it on the night he was betrayed.

I didn't pretend to know the path forward. I didn't even share optimism for a united Church. I just talked about my meeting with the pope and about him as a person. I shared the confession of faith he shared with me. I told the church we didn't have a plan moving forward. We don't have any projects or initiatives lined up. What we are committed to doing is praying. This would be a Holy-Spirit-guided endeavor through and through.

And the church stood up and cheered.

As I told the story in each service over the weekend, thousands of people were excited about unity in the Church. More excited than I dared to hope.

So how can I be a part of this? That's the real question, right? That's what my church body wanted to know. That's what pastors ask when they hear the story. The call is simple. The language and direction have been evolving and getting simpler. But here is what I tell people.

Pray daily. Pray for unity in your local church body. Pray for unity in the churches in your community. Pray for unity in the Church globally.

Fellowship monthly. Once a month, go out to lunch or coffee with someone outside of your Christian tribe. Get to know them as a person. Don't debate theology but share the difference Jesus has made in your life and how important he is to you.

Too simplistic? Possibly. Will individuals praying daily and developing friendships mend five hundred years of division? To be honest, I don't stand confident in that plan. What I stand confident in is the Holy Spirit. When we pray, God listens. He does the miraculous, starting in our own hearts and relationships. When we develop new relationships with other believers, the Holy Spirit is present. He will guide and direct. He will prompt initiatives to start and programs to develop. I don't know what is going to happen in the area of unity. I don't know what the thing is that will bring us together. But God does.

God desires unity, so I desire unity. My prayer for you is that you will pursue it as well.

117

To Love Is to Serve

Ken Costa

Thursday, June 8, 2017, was a day that I will never forget. The noise and the bustle of conversation was long gone, and had given way to silent expectation. Two rows of leaders from a myriad of backgrounds and denominations were gathered around one chair that soon would be occupied by Pope Francis. Everybody's attention was centered on the doors through which he would enter. In a few short minutes, all eyes would be focused on the now-empty chair. We would have the privilege of spending two hours with the pope, asking him questions, hearing his answers, and spending time up close with a man whom most see only from a distance.

By no means was our excitement caused by the opulence of the occasion or a room decorated with the regalia and emblems that are often associated with people of such authority. Instead, what struck me was the simplicity of the room in which we were gathered. It was a small, unassuming, modern room deep in the heart of the Vatican that stood in stark contrast to the towering externals that we often see. This was a theme woven into the fabric of our visit. As I waited in those final few moments for the pope to arrive, the simplicity and humility of the surroundings reminded me of the previous twenty-four hours our group had spent together.

It was unlike anything I'd experienced before. We had gathered in the grounds of Castel Gandolfo, the summer residence of the pope, and listened to Giovanni, a Pentecostal pastor, speak to us about Christ's washing the disciples' feet.

His words were simple yet charged with power and meaning: "If you truly want to serve someone do not start with the head. Take the lesson from Christ: start from the feet. This is the great lesson of reconciliation." Little did I know what would come next . . .

I had always tried to imagine what it must have been like for the disciples. It had been a long day. Jerusalem was packed with Passover pilgrims, and as the disciples took their places around the supper table, Jesus took the initiative as he always did. I've meditated on Jesus' picking up a servant's cord and placing it around his waste, on his picking up the bowl and kneeling before each one of the disciples. It has always been staggering to me how, one after the other, Jesus worked his way down his row of friends—the same hands that flung stars into space, now cleansing his friends' dirty feet, even Judas's. In the ultimate act of humility, hours before his own death, he wanted his friends to understand how much he cared for them. But never could I have imagined that I would have the opportunity to participate in a reenactment of that upper room scene as each of us washed one another's feet. It not only brought the scene to life but also encouraged us to embrace a virtue that often escapes us: humility. I am so grateful to have had the privilege of being invited to be part of this extraordinary gathering of reconcilers.

Then it all happened, a most remarkable moment. As Pope Francis entered the room, his presence was unassuming. He moved slowly, slightly stooped but not bowed, reflecting a man in his early eighties. His eyes glistened, accentuated by the traditional white papal cassock and wooden cross which hung around his neck. I was struck by the serenity of his face, and the purpose behind his walk. He surprised us by making his way to greet the people in the back row first. It was a small but significant gesture, modeling the humility that has become the chief cornerstone of his papacy.

I continued to watch him with a sense of admiration. His actions reflected a depth of spirituality that was clearly a result of his own dependence on God to accomplish the work he has been called to carry out. He kept asking us, one by one, to pray for him. It was a constant refrain over the time we had together. I was struck that such a man, who is in a position of nearly unlimited power and authority, was so genuinely dependent on prayer.

From the start of his papacy, Pope Francis has chosen one simple phrase to describe both his personal leadership style and the attitude he wishes to engender within the Church: "humility in action." He does not just pay lip service to the concept; it is imbued deep within his every action. As he began to address us in Italian, he unequivocally told us that he was not going to give us a sermon. It emphasized the desire of a man who did not want to be measured by the words which he said, but rather the works he carried out. This is indeed where Pope Francis shines. He looked at every one of our faces with compassion and tenderness; to him every face was special. Every face had a story. He was modeling something so rare in our contemporary culture. When we see a big crowd, we see exactly that, a crowd, filling an arena or flooding a shopping center. We see people, not persons as individuals, but people. But Pope Francis not only embraced every question with dignity, but also the person asking the question.

I have chosen to reflect on this "humility in action" mandate that Pope Francis exhibited both in his interactions with us and in the words he shared during our time together. In particular, I would like to draw out three examples that demonstrate well the love he conveyed.

First, Pope Francis displayed humility in action as he described why he decided not to live in the palatial papal apartments, the prospect of which many a good leader would become enamored by. Instead, he chose to live very simply, in the Casa Santa Marta, which can almost be likened to a bed and breakfast. Not only did he feel as though he would be overwhelmed by the palace, but he loves to be where people are. It felt as though Pope Francis was presenting us with a new option where community and love for others take center stage. An option where we take the lowest place, not the highest, seeking to serve, not to be served. Life can often make hermits out of us, driving us into isolation. Driven by our own needs and wants, we forget that the courage we need can be found through community and fellowship. It is here that our hope is fed, in a community of believers fostered where we live, where we work, and where we worship.

Though he loves people, Francis was not unrealistic about the tensions and strains brought about through relationship with others. He was thoughtful on the subject of tension and pressure in the world. There is no escape from reality, he said. So we should not think that we can escape the tensions in the world. They are similar to those faced by Jesus. However, Jesus' final prayer before the cross in John chapter 17 was for the unity of all. Would he offer a prayer that couldn't be answered? "Human beings make for disagreement but cannot make peace," the pope said. "Peace is a gift from God and something we should all strive for."

The second example of humility in action is how movingly he spoke about his election as pope. He described how he went into the small room, sometimes called the Room of Tears, adjoining the Sistine Chapel (where the conclave was held). In what was going to be one of the most defining moments in his life, he prayed but did not shed tears. He believed that there was a calling on his life. His close friend, a cardinal sitting next to him in the conclave, had whispered to him immediately upon his election, "Never forget the poor." This was his dominant thought as he prayed alone in the chapel. Francis told us that when we come across the poor and the marginalized it is easy to reach out and drop a coin in a bucket and then rapidly withdraw our hand. Instead he urged us to keep our hands outstretched, and instead of retracting them, to touch the person and stay to affirm their humanity: "Do not underestimate a physical touch; it establishes a common humanity." It reminded me that none of us can do everything but each of us can do something.

Even amidst the scope of his influence, and the position of authority he holds, he wants to embody Jesus' "Nazareth Manifesto": "The Spirit of the Lord is upon me, because he has anointed me to bring good news to the poor. He has sent me to proclaim release to the captives and recovery of sight to the blind, to let the oppressed go free" (Luke 4:18).

For Pope Francis, compassion seems to be the best apologetic. He repeatedly urged us to remember that mercy is the hallmark of Christianity. He went on to say, "In reaching out to the marginalized, look them in the eyes rather than darting away. And in doing so reflect the compassion of Christ in human terms." The value of every human life and every human story, especially the lives and stories of the poor, is central to our Christian life. Compassion is an aspect of love, and represents real attention to people's needs and a desire to meet people where they are. Pope Francis went on to lament the mindset of our modern society and its priorities. He urged us "not to abandon our humanity for the sake of economic prosperity."

Thirdly, I was drawn to the pope's response when someone asked what the most important requirement of modern life is. He immediately gestured to his ear: "Listening." For him, nothing is more important in a noisy world: listening to the cries of the poor, the world, and those without hope. For many of us, listening doesn't happen by default; therefore it must happen by design. To him, listening is the tool we need to make reconciliation possible. And he asked us to never forget Jesus' words: "For I was hungry and you gave me food, I was thirsty and you gave me something to drink, I was a stranger and you welcomed me, I was naked and you gave me clothing, I was sick and you took care of me, I was in prison and you visited me" (Matthew 25:35-36).

The practice and discipline of listening undergirds Pope Francis's entire ministry. When asked about the work of the Holy Spirit his eyes lit up. He spoke movingly of the Holy Spirit as a flow in our lives. He encouraged us to tune *in* to the convicting voice of the Holy Spirit and tune *out* the condemning voices that can surround us on a daily basis.

It was clear to me that Pope Francis finds the strength to do what he does by being totally open to the Holy Spirit, to the newness of the work of the Holy Spirit, and the creativity of how the Spirit moves, and by embracing the character of the Holy Spirit as the Spirit of God. His love for the Holy Spirit is made evident by his cooperation with the Spirit. In a homily in April 2013, he said, "The Holy Spirit annoys us, because he moves us, he makes us travel, he pushes the Church forward."[8] This openness to the Holy Spirit was clearly demonstrated by his desire for the John 17 Movement to be birthed. As the Lord's works are ever new, the creativity of the Holy Spirit produces ever richer diversity, creating a unity that is never uniformity but multifaceted in its nature.

As the two hours came to a close, Pope Francis got up, and as he left the room, he shook all our hands and indulged us with selfies. My overriding memory is of the spiritual depth reflected in his eyes, the astonishing humility of a man who carries more weight than I can imagine, and yet who treated us as if we were the most important people in the world. When asked by Joseph at an earlier point whether we should bring the audience to a close, he looked at him and asked, "Do you have an airplane to catch?" He was clearly enjoying his time with us and didn't want it to end.

I walked away from this rich and memorable occasion recognizing the diversity within the Church and the beautiful unity the Holy Spirit creates. In this time we got a glimpse into the transformative power of humility in action by meeting Pope Francis. It is the humility he lives by, that enables him to treat all people with dignity and respect. I am inspired and challenged to do the same in my own life, and in my interactions with others, both like and different from me.

---

8. Pope Francis, "Morning Meditation in the Chapel of the *Domus Sanctae Marthae*," April 16, 2013. http://w2.vatican.va/content/francesco/en/cotidie/2013/documents/papa-francesco-cotidie_20130416_spirit.html.

To kneel as Jesus knelt, picking up my washbasin, humbling myself, and washing people's feet with love, kindness, and mercy is as memorable a part of the visit as meeting the pope.

Finding Strength

Mark Buckley

There are two things every great marriage, church, friendship, and business have in common. The first is unity. Unity helps make marriages fulfilling, churches fruitful, friendships joyful, and businesses productive. The second thing they have in common is imperfect people. Imperfect people can be selfish, hurtful, and a pain to be around. Therefore, to have unity with imperfect people, we must learn how to overcome selfish and hurtful behavior. Fortunately, Jesus Christ can teach us how to love and forgive each other so we can live in unity. If Jesus is the Lord of our lives, and he tells us unity is his will, then unity is possible, even with imperfect people.

This is the short version of how I found unity in the most important areas of my life.

As a child, I was taught that our Church was the only true church. Our Church boasted the most Christians and the biggest and best church buildings. Our bishops were appointed by the pope himself—a direct successor of the apostle Peter. We had the only true experience of the Body of Christ when we celebrated the Mass on Sundays and partook of the Eucharist. No other Christians had the blessings and gifts of our Church. I had no reason to doubt what I had been taught for a long time.

My dad was an only child who was raised Catholic. He attended Catholic schools from grade school through college. My mother was raised Episcopalian. She was so impressed with my father's commitment to the Church that she converted to Catholicism after I was born.

I attended catechism classes every week during the school year from first grade through my junior year of high school. I believed in Jesus Christ and felt especially close to the Lord when I received the Eucharist. I went to confession every few weeks so that I could partake in Communion with a clear conscience.

Our family attended Mass every Sunday, even on vacation. One winter weekend, we went skiing with my godfather and his family. We were caught in a major snowstorm at Lake Tahoe. The snow was so deep that we couldn't drive to the nearest Catholic church for Mass. So my dad and godfather took our families to an Episcopal church just a block away. They told us it was the closest thing to a Catholic church and the Lord would understand our situation.

I was in high school at the time, and it was my first experience attending a different kind of church. The building was nice, but not as nice as our church back home. The service was a little longer than the thirty-five-minute Mass I was accustomed to. The communion wafer tasted different. The liturgy used familiar words, but it wasn't the same. I was intrigued, but not overly impressed, with my first venture outside our tradition. The most memorable effect of this experience was the comment, "The Lord will understand our situation." It seemed liberating.

One evening, when I was sixteen years old, I asked my catechism teacher a question about God. He replied, "That is a mystery." Then he continued his lecture. I thought, "If it is a mystery to you, and a mystery to me, I'm going to go somewhere where I can find some answers." That was my last catechism class. After that night, my attendance at Sunday Mass became sporadic. My parents let me make my own decision about church attendance once I turned sixteen, and I chose to go other places.

For the next couple of years, I was deeply involved in the sex, drugs, and rock and roll scene in San Francisco and Marin County. For me, college was a continual party, until I had a breakdown at nineteen years of age. I was admitted to a mental institution for four months and experienced deep depression for the first time in my life. But I also began to pray to the Lord again.

After graduating from high school, one of my good friends had committed his life to Jesus Christ. He began to share his faith with me after my breakdown. I soon met others who were involved in the Jesus Movement that was sweeping through California in 1969. Young people heard the gospel from hippies who had forsaken drugs and boldly shared their faith. They handed out gospel tracts and sang songs in local parks. Bible studies were full of kids with long hair, beads, and bell-bottoms.

I had been intrigued by Jesus ever since I was a child. If Jesus was alive, like my friend and the others said, then I knew I wanted to get to know him. I didn't know if I could stay away from marijuana and immorality for the rest of my life, so I struggled with my decision. One night before going to sleep, I decided to take the step I had avoided. I knelt beside my bed and prayed. I asked Jesus to come into my heart and be my Lord and Savior. I felt a little peace. I was no longer running away from the Lord.

After that night, I started to read the Bible for the first time in my life. I began to attend Bible studies in homes packed with young people who were singing, praying aloud, and giving testimonies. At first, I was uncomfortable, because praying from your heart and quoting scripture were new to me. But I wanted to get to know Jesus, so I kept returning to the meetings.

For the first time in my life I began to experience the grace of God. My pattern of guilt and shame for failing to live a life that was pleasing to the Lord was broken. While reading the Bible and praying I found power to overcome sin.

I started attending Tuesday night Bible studies led by a former Baptist pastor who opened his home to teach Jesus People (members of the Jesus Movement). I visited Friday night Catholic charismatic meetings where hundreds of people sang and worshiped the Lord in prayer. On Sundays I attended various churches.

Every church I visited was unique, but each offered something special about Jesus. I felt the power of God in the Assembly of God Church. There was dynamic worship at the non-denominational church. The Baptists had great Bible teaching. I felt God's peace and enjoyed Communion in the Catholic Masses. At the Church of God in Christ, the love of the African American community was heartwarming.

I thought about returning to the Catholic Church permanently. However, I had a better connection with the Lord in the simple Bible studies I was attending. I preferred simplicity and spontaneity to liturgy. I wanted to follow Jesus with all my heart. I didn't want to spend my life trying to reform an institution.

After a couple of years, I became one of several leaders of the Jesus People. Our Bible studies grew throughout Marin and Sonoma Counties. We borrowed fellowship halls from Presbyterian churches, Methodist churches, and the Church of God to hold our weekly meetings. We started Christian general stores in San Rafael, Novato, Petaluma, San Francisco, and Sonoma. In these stores we sold Bibles and Christian books and music to believers throughout the area. We tried to serve all the local churches.

We established numerous discipleship houses where we hosted young people who desired to grow closer to the Lord. Many of them had hitchhiked to California from around the country, searching for a new lifestyle. We gave them food and shelter and taught them about Jesus. As our ministry grew, we decided to start a church called the Church of the Open Door. We didn't think we were better than every other church—we simply wanted to provide good care for the hundreds of young people we encountered.

By 1976 our movement had grown to four churches. I was leading a congregation in Novato, California. I was twenty-six years old and knew I still had a lot to learn. I met with pastors of several local churches at a weekly fellowship lunch at a restaurant. There were Baptist pastors, a couple of Lutheran ministers, a Catholic priest, an Episcopalian priest, a Methodist pastor, and two Presbyterian ministers who met regularly for lunch, prayer, and discussions.

One week someone suggested we pair up and schedule a "pulpit exchange." I asked Fr. John, the Catholic priest from Our Lady of Loreto Parish, if he would like to preach at our morning services at the Church of the Open Door. He gladly accepted and invited me to speak at an upcoming special service at Our Lady of Loreto.

On the appointed Sunday, Fr. John arrived wearing a black shirt and clerical collar. I usually dressed more casually, so it was a different, but not unfamiliar, look for the young people in our congregation. Many of our members had been raised Catholic but had left the Church in their teenage years. I introduced Fr. John to the congregation after our praise and worship time. He preached a message about the love of God. Our church was blessed and encouraged by his faith and love for Jesus.

In the second week of January 1980, I spoke at Our Lady of Loreto. Several members of Open Door accompanied me. Fr. John asked me to speak from Matthew chapter 3 about the baptism of Jesus, the Gospel reading in the Catholic Lectionary for that day. It was special for me to give my first message in a Catholic Church on the fullness of the Holy Spirit. I had just turned 30 years old—and I knew Jesus was baptized when he was 30.

Incense permeated the sanctuary, songs of praise were sung to the Lord, and then I got up to preach. When my message ended, everyone sat in silence for several minutes. At first, I thought I must have offended Fr. John and he didn't know what to do. Later, I realized he sat in silence as a sign of respect and reflection on the message. That day I experienced how different traditions show respect and appreciation in unique ways.

Besides the weekly lunches I attended in Novato, I joined a group of pastors from many denominations in a fellowship called United Bay Area Ministers. We met monthly to pray together and share wisdom for the ministry challenges we faced. God honored the time I invested in these relationships. I was busy with our young family and a growing church. Some months I was tempted to skip the meetings. However, over the years we became friends. We prayed together for our churches and our nation.

I learned lessons from those meetings that are still with me today. I discovered that every denomination has spiritual gifts and strengths, just like individuals have gifts and strengths. I gained fresh insights into scripture passages shared by those from different backgrounds. These relationships enriched my life and strengthened me for the ministry.

John chapter 17 has been a motivating passage of scripture for me since I was ordained in 1974. John 17:21 shows that unity is Jesus' priority because it enables us to accomplish his purposes. Jesus wants the world to know he was sent here by the Father and that we too are loved by the Father. He prays that we will be in unity so these truths can be revealed to the world.

Since 1984, I have worked with pastors and leaders to build bridges of unity in the Body of Christ in the Phoenix area. Over the years, our church has benefited greatly from these relationships. When Living Streams, a church I founded, has been in need, leaders from other ministries have come and given our elders wisdom and counsel. These relationships have helped me through personal crisis as well.

On Sunday night, May 31, 1992, my wife Kristina and I were hosting a new home group. To help everyone get to know each other better, I asked them to share their favorite scripture. In the middle of the meeting, our sixteen-year-old son Matthew came home. I invited him to join us and share his favorite scripture. Matthew said his favorite scripture passage was Philippians 2:1-2.

We opened our Bibles while Matthew read, "If then there is any encouragement in Christ, any consolation from love, any sharing in the Spirit, any compassion and sympathy, make my joy complete: be of the same mind, having the same love, being in full accord and of one mind." I thought it was an interesting scripture for him to choose, but it didn't really impact me until a few weeks later.

Matthew finished his junior year of high school that week. The next day, to celebrate getting out of school, he and eight other friends went tubing down the Salt River, an hour's drive east of Phoenix. Matthew was safety conscious and a good swimmer, he loved the Lord, and none of his friends drank or did drugs. I had no apprehension about his trip.

The kids went tubing in the hot sun for a couple of hours. Then, to cool off, Matthew playfully fell out of his tube at a bend in the river. Beneath him a vortex had been created by unusually high water from spring runoff pressing against a rock wall. Matthew was pinned underwater against the rock wall. It took twenty minutes and a sheriff's boat to pull him out of the water. The paramedics revived his heart, but his brain was destroyed. He died three days later in the hospital.

Kristina and I were devastated by the loss of our first-born son.

Friends and family came to comfort us. Pastors and leaders from all parts of the Body of Christ shared their love and supported us. We had big memorial services to honor Matthew in Arizona and California that were organized and funded by leaders who loved us.

In the weeks after Matthew's death, while my heart was still grieving, I reread his favorite scripture, Philippians 2:1-2, many times. It was Matthew's final message to me. It was a message on the priority of unity. The apostle Paul was basically saying, "If you are getting anything at all out of your relationship with Jesus, then please be united in mind and heart with your brothers in Christ."

I looked up other passages, like 1 Corinthians 1:10 and Romans 15:5-6, that also make it clear that unity in our relationships is the Lord's priority. We glorify God when we are in unity together. We discover his wisdom and experience his blessings when we are united in love. Yet I had to admit I was not a good example of living in unity in the closest relationships in my life.

I loved my wife, but I often insisted we do things my way, regardless of her feelings. As a leader at our church I sometimes pressed our other pastors and elders to yield to my wishes, even when they felt differently. I was a strong leader, and I knew how to get what I wanted, but my leadership style often put stress on those closest to me. Over the next few years, I made a shift in my approach to leadership.

I realized unity in our marriage was more important than whatever I might feel was the best immediate decision for our family. I decided that unity with our elders and leaders was more important than my being right about decisions our church faced. I wasn't always consistent in this new approach, but the change in my priorities brought blessings I didn't anticipate.

Kristina began to enjoy our marriage more. As a result, the pain we experienced over Matthew's death became a redemptive grace in our lives. Our leaders at Living Streams felt better working with me. Our church was blessed with a new grace that enabled us to grow and expand year by year. People came to Christ, and we planted new churches. I discovered that unity is God's priority because it brings blessings in every area of life.

I joined the John 17 Movement soon after it began in Phoenix in 2015. It reminded me of the unity movement I was involved with in the 1970s. God's plan has not changed over the years. At times, however, the Holy Spirit moves in ways that emphasize different truths. The Lord seems to be reemphasizing unity today.

It was a special privilege for me to join the leaders of John 17 for meetings with Pope Francis in June 2017. We were welcomed into the apostolic palace, one of the most beautiful buildings in the world, for the first meeting. Our second meeting took place in the chapel of his residence. The chapel was not ornate, but our experience as a group was even more powerful.

The sixty of us with John 17 came from many different denominations. We prayed with Pope Francis, sang together, and asked him questions for two hours. If you were to read a transcript of our conversation without knowing who was answering our questions, you would have never guessed we were talking with the leader of the Roman Catholic Church.

The transcript would not contain references to Church synods or quotes from Church Fathers. It would be obvious, however, that we were talking to a man who loved Jesus Christ and knew the Word of God, because Pope Francis quoted the words of Jesus continually. It would also be apparent that we were asking questions of a man who was humble, because Pope Francis often finished statements with the phrase, "Of course, that is just my opinion."

And it is just my opinion that unity in the Body of Christ is possible if we love Jesus Christ and love one another. Sure, there are people who emphasize the differences between believers rather than the priorities of John chapter 17. In 1 Corinthians 11:19, Paul said, "Indeed, there have to be factions among you, for only so will it become clear who among you are genuine." There are differences among Christians. Some differences are significant, but other differences simply emphasize a unique aspect of the majesty of Christ.

There will be a day when the Lord will return, and the brightness of his glory will enable us all to see more clearly, face to face (see 1 Corinthians 13:8-12). In the meantime, there is more to be gained through unity and love in the Body of Christ than is accomplished by criticism.

Pope Francis received our John 17 group as brothers and sisters in Christ, without regard to our denominational affiliations. His welcome made me feel like my life had come full circle. The Lord didn't need me to reform an institution. Jesus is the head of the Church and he perfects it as he chooses. The Lord has given me the freedom to serve him as I feel is best. The churches I have helped establish are not perfect, nor can they be truly healthy apart from the rest of the Body of Christ. I'm grateful for those who receive us in Christ. We need each other to be whole.

My life is focused on building mature leaders and establishing healthy churches. I believe all our churches will be healthier if we work in unity with other leaders who love Jesus. If a local church is connected to other churches in unity, then the resources Jesus has placed throughout his Body are able to flow to that church. Unity allows the life of Christ to flow freely to each of us, giving us grace, and enabling us to bear more fruit and glorify God.

What's not to like about that?

A Common Hymnal

Matt Maher

In August of 2005, I read the news of the passing of Brother Roger, the founder of the Taizé community. Taizé is an ecumenical community of brothers in France who have a charism of meditatively singing repetitive phrases. Brother Roger was a monk from the Reformed Church who witnessed the transformative power of sung prayer. After the Second Vatican Council, he began to bear witness more and more to the very real work of unity that the Holy Spirit was orchestrating in the midst of worship. In 1980, at St. Peter's Basilica, he said, "I have found my own identity as a Christian by reconciling within myself the faith of my origins with the mystery of the Catholic faith, without breaking fellowship with anyone."[9]

Reading about this as a young musician with a desire to write congregational music was like discovering another branch in my family tree. I realized I belong to a rich heritage of people who were burdened by the very real and urgent request of Jesus to his Father that we would be one as he and the Father are one. So I embarked on a new assignment from the Lord. It is in and of itself an "Emmaus road" of encounter that I am still walking to this day. It is that type of encounter I see active in the movement of John 17: Jesus walking with us in our joys and disappointments and revealing himself active in our lives, which in turn leads

---

9. "Something that was without precedent," Taizé, last modified April 12, 2008. https://www.taize.fr/en_article6739.html.

to a greater desire for intimacy and friendship with the Lord and with each other.

In such a divided time, is that goal even possible? Not only is it possible, I have come to realize more and more it is of paramount importance to the mission of the Church in the world. The first time I read that testimony from Brother Roger, my heart leapt out of my chest. I distinctly sensed Jesus telling me, "This is the torch I want you to carry with your life." That same month, I signed a deal with a large Christian music publisher. I realized that Jesus wanted me to be in fellowship among Christians from other denominations so that I could come to know him more and appreciate the gift that Jesus gives in the larger Church as the Body of Christ. The main motivation in my discernment and in my decision was the seventeenth chapter of John's Gospel—Jesus' prayer for unity.

The following January, I stood on the floor of a stadium in Nashville and heard 11,000 college students sing a song I had written while working at a Catholic parish in Mesa, Arizona, years before. The overwhelming thought I had at the time was the realization that up to that point I had not cared about any of these fellow believers because they didn't go to the same kind of church that I did. My heart broke simultaneously to a new reality and for a new possibility.

I started down this "Emmaus road" of fellowship and encountering Jesus in the midst of writing songs and praying with other worship leaders and Christian artists, but more importantly, we had wonderful fellowship and friendship. It seems that in younger generations of believers there aren't as many hang-ups. There are no agendas, just the love and pursuit of Jesus; and in that space of humble fellowship, God commands a blessing. To me, all the songs I've been part of writing aren't about the songs themselves. They are about the Lord and the friendships and moments of prayer together that we experienced in the creative process. I've always felt that the blessing of unity was embedded in the songs themselves; it is as if God uses the context of the modern world to create a common hymnal of music.

Walking the Emmaus road of unity isn't without hardship. I remember leading worship at a festival outside of London in 2008, and hearing the Holy Spirit say to me, "If you want to be a bridge, you're gonna have to lay down and let people walk all over you." It was a very honest revelation from the Spirit of God! But you have to have the courage to not flinch when you feel the "sting" of disunity. At some point, your friendships feel like family, and with family can come arguments and disagreements. But when you both know you're not going to walk away from your friendship, you can have the difficult conversations. True friendship sows the seeds of a willingness to sit in those moments of tension and not sugarcoat the pains and hurts Christians have caused one another, or the tensions found in our differences.

This is evident even in my own family life. My wife Kristin grew up Methodist. We live out the call to relational reconciliation in our marriage and family by attending two different church communities in Nashville. Nowhere is this more painfully obvious than in the Eucharist, when we both experience the sting of not receiving Communion in one another's congregations. These moments are better endured with deep purpose when held simultaneously with the foundational commonalities we all share, and in the all-too-important context of community. Jesus is still forever united to the Father and the Spirit, and to his Church, and therein lies the promise of hope. This is where the mission and movement of John 17 has intersected with my own life and calling in such a timely way.

When I first heard there was a movement emerging of pastors from different denominations coming together for prayer and fellowship, I was so encouraged. When I heard that it echoed a huge burden in the heart of Pope Francis, I was emboldened in a way I hadn't been before. As a Catholic, there have been times when the endeavor of pursuing unity in the Church has felt like a lonely one. There are many pressing matters in the life of the Church these days, and with the advent of social media, many distractions. With an ever-increasing obsession with politics, many Christians focus so much on observation and criticism of every event that pops up on their newsfeed that they are lulled into complacency about things that are actually changeable. Disunity is changeable because unity starts with family and friendship—unity starts with relationship! Imagine the possibilities—how different the world would be if Christians were a sign of unity in the midst of diversity; imagine what could be accomplished in Jesus' name!

Last June, Kristin and I joined a group of delegates who journeyed to Rome for a time of fellowship, dialogue, and prayer with Pope Francis. In an ever-increasing world of transactional activity, what we experienced with the pope was *transformational* activity. More and more, I see this element of transformation as a key sign of God's continued presence and blessing. During the meeting, a pastor asked the Holy Father one thing he would teach her children if he could. He said, "Teach your children to sing praise and worship to God. It is the purest form of prayer, especially praise: it is prayer with no self-interest. . . . So, teach them to praise and worship and they will have a relationship with God forever."

On the Emmaus road of unity, there are moments where Jesus' presence becomes so clear you get a good case of heartburn! Of course, I am not talking about indigestion. I am talking about that moment when the presence of God is so strong you are consoled and convicted all at the same time. When I heard the Holy Father share these words, I felt such an encouragement from the Holy Spirit to keep doing what I'm doing. There's a line in my song "Lord I Need You" that says:

Teach my song to rise to You when temptation comes my way

When I cannot stand I'll fall on You; Jesus, You're my hope and stay

I realize more and more in my life that the greatest temptation we face as believers is to think that prayer doesn't matter, that our song doesn't matter. But as St. Augustine says, singing is like praying twice. Singing is powerful because it involves the will and the intellect while simultaneously engaging your heart. An amazing thing happens when people sing together—they can't yell at each other! Singing gives testimony without the need for a dramatic speech. The same God who makes sweeping changes in the lives of saints and sinners makes subtle and lasting changes in each and every one of us, and singing becomes such a simple yet powerful testimony to his work.

Singing gives people permission to join in the song, and in that song is a real sense of belonging. I remember the first time I walked into a charismatic prayer meeting; I had never heard or felt anything like it before in my life. I studied music for seven years in post-secondary institutions and I've sung Palestrina in a chamber choir, but it never sounded as beautiful as the sound of people free enough in their own humanity to just spontaneously sing a song to God. That afternoon with the Holy Father as we prayed and sang, our souls lifted and were made light again in fellowship with each other and with a God who *is* a fellowship, three Persons in perfect unity. This is the promise that keeps us walking on the Emmaus road of unity.

The Canterbury Tales by Geoffrey Chaucer is a collection of pilgrims' stories on the way to Canterbury Cathedral. Chaucer originally planned to write four tales for each character: two on the way, one at the destination, and one at home. He never got to finish it. Perhaps in its state of incompleteness it is, in fact, complete. No one and nothing this side of heaven is a finished work, save the work of Jesus on the cross. We are an unfolding mystery, a mix of frailty and wonder capable of bearing witness to miracles that make the universe shudder in praise and delight. Like the pilgrims to Canterbury, we too have concerns, both temporal and eternal, and on the way, Jesus appears, revealing his heart for the reconciliation of all things.

A New Understanding of Peter

Bishop James Massa

The lead-up to my encounter with Pope Francis began in a New York diner over omelets and conversation about Jesus' prayer for unity. Joseph Tosini, an ordained pastor who mentors other pastors in the Evangelical world, found my name through a mutual friend in the Focolare Movement. "I know you have a background in Christian unity, but I want to share with you a new kind of ecumenism that's based on the methods of Pope Francis," he said. "Meet me at the Floridian Diner on Saturday. By the way, I'm bringing two friends."

The phone conversation was all of four minutes. But something about the unaffected confidence with which Joseph spoke convinced me that I needed to clear my schedule and honor his invitation. The two friends turned out to be Guy Wasko, a pastor of the dynamic Trinity Grace Church in New York City, and Julia Torres, an official from the Vatican's Pontifical Council for the Laity and a longtime friend of Pope Francis.

To break the ice, each of us shared a little of our own personal journeys as disciples deeply committed to healing divisions within the Body of Christ. I recounted my work as Executive Director of the Secretariat for Ecumenical and Interreligious Affairs at the United States Conference of Catholic Bishops (USCCB), where I helped coordinate some of the official dialogues between the Catholic Church and her Orthodox, Protestant, and Evangelical partners. The aim of this form of ecumenism is to reconcile opposing doctrines and liturgical practices that have proven to be church-dividing over the centuries. Guy spoke about his outreach to other faith communities as a New York City police chaplain. His role requires a kind of practical ecumenism based on "praying anywhere and with anyone," not to mention being a compassionate listener to officers in crisis. Drawing on her experiences of working with then-Cardinal Bergoglio in Buenos Aires, Julia reflected on the need for local initiatives in building bridges among faith communities modeled on the efforts of the pope.

On July 28, 2014, the Holy Father made what the Vatican called a "strictly private visit" to Caserta in the south of Italy to address the Pentecostal Church of the Reconciliation, a community led by his longtime friend, Giovanni Traettino. The church in which Francis met with more than four hundred Pentecostals was still under construction—a poignant reminder of the ongoing work of repairing relations among Christians. Julia recalled that many in the room wept when the pope spoke about the complicity of some Catholics in the fascist-era persecution of Italian Pentecostals and asked for their forgiveness.

These minority Christians had lived on the margins of a predominantly Catholic, and now increasingly secular, culture. Previously scorned and harshly denounced as proselytizers, the Italian Pentecostals now heard the pope—the symbol of all that had made the lives of their forebears miserable—asking them to forgive the members of his branch of the Christian family who had not lived up to Christ's teaching. The air was thick with emotion, only to be released when Francis finished his address and the assembly broke into charismatic song and prayer. "It was an unforgettable encounter with the pope," Julia said. "The Bishop of Rome came as an estranged brother and he left as a pastor to those who don't even belong to his flock."

As our omelets got cold, Joseph Tosini ordered more coffee for everyone and then began to explain how "the

Francis effect" is impacting the Evangelical and Pentecostal worlds. "Through most of the last hundred years, we've been left out of the ecumenical movement," he said. "By instinct, we Evangelicals have shied away from talk about structural unity, which is admirably the goal of organizations like the World Council of Churches. But for us, what's primary is fellowship and mission." According to Joseph, Jorge Bergoglio gets it. Ever since he was appointed archbishop of Buenos Aires in 1998, he has shown remarkable sensitivity to the perceptions and aspirations of the emergent new churches of Latin America.

On various occasions Pope Francis has spoken about an ecumenism of encounter, in which the dialogue of friendship paves the way for common witness in society and those other forms of dialogue that help remove obstacles to professing the faith in common. Like his predecessors Pope St. John Paul II and Pope Benedict XVI, Francis lauds the accomplishments of the dialogues by teams of Church leaders and scholars from Catholic, Orthodox, Anglican, and Protestant communions. Over the past fifty years, they have produced remarkable texts like the Faith and Order Commission's Report *Baptism, Eucharist and Ministry* (WCC, 1982) and the Catholic Church and Lutheran World Federation's *Joint Declaration on the Doctrine of Justification* (1999). These theological documents, and many like them generated at the international and local levels, rightly deserve our gratitude. They have brought the separated communities closer, one step at a time, to that fullness of reconciliation that Jesus wills for his Body. But they're not enough.

The growing edge of global Christianity is asking for another kind of engagement from their Catholic brothers and sisters. "We need to walk together. We need to pray together. We need to *accompany* one another in ministry." This was Joseph's appeal, as he shared his conviction that the Holy Spirit is accomplishing a new work through the actions of Pope Francis and his allies like Pastor Traettino.

Preceding the 2016 visit of John 17 to Rome, pastors, priests, and lay colleagues began to meet regularly in Phoenix, Arizona. Joseph called on several key contacts whose engagement with the project would give it credibility within the Evangelical world. Mike Herron, Robert Briggs, and Gary Kinnaman were ready to take a fresh look at Jesus' final prayer in John chapter 17, when he called upon his Father to keep his disciples—and all those who would come after them—in the fellowship of trinitarian love that has bound the Father with the Son from all eternity. "How can we refuse trying to answer Christ's prayer that we be one?" Joseph pleaded.

Calls were made to local parishes. Networks within the Charismatic Renewal and other Catholic groups with a track record of interfacing with Evangelicals were tapped. On the Catholic side, Auxiliary Bishop Eduardo Nevares, Peter and Sharon Poppleton, and Matteo Calisi came forward with the encouragement of the Catholic bishop of Phoenix, Thomas Olmsted, who had been a member of the USCCB Committee on Ecumenical and Interreligious Affairs. What began tentatively as a series of discussions over lunch evolved into overnight retreats and visits to one another's houses of worship. Bonds of fellowship began to reach into other cities, as word began to spread about a new movement called John 17.

"We'd like to see it plant roots here in Brooklyn," Joseph finally revealed at our breakfast meeting. The choice of Brooklyn and its contiguous New York City borough of Queens—as Guy Wasko well understood—makes sense, given the revitalization of the region in recent years, owing to the influx of hipsters and new immigrants from countries in Asia and Africa where the Christian presence is that of a tiny minority. What better place for Catholics with long-established parishes and Evangelicals with vital new centers of worship to engage in a process of fellowship-building and witnessing together to the gospel we hold in common?

Joseph had one other piece of news. "By the way, we're also planning another sit-down with Pope Francis in June, and you're invited." My immediate reaction was to demur while explaining that as an auxiliary bishop, I would need to obtain various permissions to participate in such an ecumenical gathering. "I have our episcopal conference to consult. My own diocesan bishop would need to approve of my absence from the diocese. And that's Confirmation season!" No matter what excuses I presented, Joseph laughed all the harder. "Don't you want to answer the prayer of Jesus? Pope Francis wants you there—I have it on good authority."

We all parted amiably and with promises to remain in touch. The following week, a surprising letter arrived in the mail. The Pontifical Council for Interreligious Dialogue (PCID), to which I had been a consultor since 2008, announced that a plenary meeting of the council would be convened the week of June 5, 2017. I reached for my smartphone to check my calendar for the date on which the second meeting of John 17 with the pope was scheduled: it was June 8. So as Providence would have it, I would be in Rome anyway. I immediately phoned Joseph to tell him of the coincidence, and on the other end I heard only laughter. "So, you have me," I said. "But we have lots more to talk about as the visit gets closer."

The juxtaposition of my two meetings at the Vatican struck me as ironic. Even though both meetings can be considered an extension of the Church's mission to unity, they could not be more different in style and substance. The PCID is a gathering of Catholic bishops and scholars to discuss the state of interreligious relations around the world, with special emphasis on the regions where religion plays a role in inciting violence. The participants sit around a large conference table with individual microphones and headsets for listening to simultaneous translations. The Cardinal-President, Jean-Louis Tauran, presides over discussions that usually follow a presentation by a scholar from one of the Roman universities who is an expert on the topic under consideration. At the end of three days of discussions, Cardinal Tauran leads the council members and consultors to the apostolic palace for a formal address by the Holy Father. After the address, each participant is presented to the pope for a brief greeting and official photograph. The plenary meeting is a carefully scripted affair, and yet has a historically valid purpose in refining the Church's efforts to partner with the world's religions in advancing peace and intercultural understanding.

The John 17 encounter with Pope Francis would follow a very different format. Julia had indicated that this year's meeting would be in a similar informal setting to the first, absent all papal protocols. The group made up of mostly Evangelicals would arrive in Rome a few days early to tour the city and visit Castel Gandolfo, the historic summer residence of popes that has a palpably retreat-like atmosphere. Together with Pastor Traettino, the group would also travel to the Mariapolis Center of the Focolare Movement. There they would hear stories of many who walk the journey of Christian unity, including Focolare president Maria Voce and a few of her closest collaborators. A highlight of this trip would be a ceremony of washing one another's feet, a ritual that shows how unity begins with the feet (as in walking together) and not the head (as in theological discussions). At the end of this enriching encounter, the group would enjoy a gelato and stroll along the beach of Lake Albano.

As the day of encounter with Pope Francis approached, I began to reflect on how the papacy has been evolving in this pontificate. Catholics refer to his office as the Petrine ministry, believing that the bishops of Rome have a responsibility analogous to that given by Jesus to the apostle Peter in Matthew 16:13-19. What the pope teaches—his *Magisterium*—becomes a standard for all Catholics. Those whom the pope recognizes as validly ordained and licitly appointed to local churches act as pastors within the one Catholic network of communion. Popes are not kings, though in the past they sometimes acquired monarchical traits. Primarily, they are shepherds who are told from the day of their election that they must act in imitation of the Good Shepherd who "lays down his life for the sheep" (John 10:11).

But like everything else in the Church, the papal office has evolved over time, even as it has remained faithful in substance to the task of guaranteeing unity in the one faith. Change in the exercise of the ministry is something that even recent popes have declared to be indispensable if the one sitting on the *cathedra* (chair) of Peter is going to fulfill his mission in a world marred by so many divisions. Pope John Paul II, now elevated to the status of "St. John Paul II," wrote an encyclical in 1995 that has become the magna carta for Catholic ecumenism. In paragraphs 95 and 96 of *Ut Unum Sint* ("May They All Be One," from John 17:21), the Polish pope invites other Christians to help him—and by implication, his successors—find a way of exercising the universal care for all the Churches that renounces nothing of what is essential to its mission (as based in the Word of God), but is nonetheless open to the new situation of our day. John Paul humbly acknowledges that such a rethinking of his office is a burden that he and his fellow Catholics cannot bear alone. Dialogue with the rest of the Christian family is needed to help shape a new expression of the role of Peter in the Church.

The day of encounter with Peter finally arrived. On the morning of June 8, my dialogue with the PCID concluded on a note of gratitude and hope. Cardinal Tauran brought the plenary meeting to an end by acknowledging the courage of the bishops in attendance from the lands of the Middle East, northern Nigeria, and parts of Asia. These bishops had spoken passionately over the course of our deliberations about the persecutions of their faithful at the hands of forces that misuse religion to incite hatred of the other. Rather than turn inward, they pledged to redouble their efforts at dialogue with the leaders of other religions for the sake of defending, on behalf of all inhabitants of their lands, human dignity and human rights—including the right to practice a religion of one's choosing.

Buoyed by this meeting, I was eager to rejoin the now fifty Christian brothers and sisters who were pursuing a different kind of peacemaking. At around 2:00 p.m., we assembled in the lobby of our hotel to either taxi or walk to the Piazza del Sant'Uffizio. Near the checkpoint for entering Vatican City, plainclothes Swiss Guards awaited our arrival to escort us to the back of the Aula Paolo VI, the Paul VI Audience Hall. Inside a large parlor room with chairs positioned in an oval shape, we sat down and awaited the pope's arrival.

As Francis entered the room with Giovanni Traettino at his side, the usual applause ensued. But instead of going to a designated chair as protocol would dictate, the Holy Father went around the circle shaking hands with each participant and asking them what U.S. city they called home. Joseph then started the conversation with some general questions about how the Bishop of Rome understands his own election and his role as pastor for over a billion Christians.

The time flew by. For two hours, the pastors and their spouses asked questions of the pope that covered a vast array of issues challenging our congregations in the United States and how John 17 might allow for collaboration in meeting those challenges. The lively conversation was interrupted at various moments with spontaneous praying and singing (one pastor brought along his guitar). Joseph read from scripture. When not answering a question, or when listening to a comment made by someone else, the pope closed his eyes and appeared to enter deeply into prayer. After the group sang "Amazing Grace," Francis asked for another song. One question that resonated powerfully with many was posed by a pastor and mother, who asked the Holy Father how she might instruct her five-year-old daughter about prayer. The pope said to her, "Teach her to pray without asking for anything." The mother's voice cracked as she thanked the pope for the insight that children too can learn to love God for who God is—that is, gratuitously—and not simply for what he can do for us.

The Holy Father seemed not to want to end the session. But finally, my episcopal colleague, Auxiliary Bishop Peter Smith of Portland, asked that we allow Pope Francis to retire after spending such a generous amount of time with us. Even as the pope exited, after once more shaking hands with each participant and taking a few "unofficial" photographs, the group lingered outside the room, recounting what they had heard and how they felt the presence of the Holy Spirit in this extraordinary encounter with the Bishop of Rome.

In the Apostolic Exhortation *Evangelii Gaudium* (*The Joy of the Gospel*) that set the course for his pontificate, Pope Francis made a strong connection between the ecumenical journey and the unfinished work of evangelization. We Christians of differing confessions must learn to journey alongside one another and put aside all suspicion and distrust, he declared. Divisions within the Body of Christ are a scandal to those who have yet to receive the gospel, especially in lands ravaged by violence. Enough is enough. Evangelicals, Pentecostals, and Catholics must work together to become a leaven of peace in the wider human family. "If we really believe in the abundantly free working of the Holy Spirit, we can learn so much from one another! It is not just about being better informed about others, but rather about reaping what the Spirit has sown in them, which is also meant to be a gift for us" (*Evangelii Gaudium*, paragraph 246).

The movement John 17 affords Christians of all backgrounds extraordinary new opportunities for sharing the gifts that will allow others to come to know Jesus, the way, the truth, and the life. By the grace of God, Peter has found a new role to play in this endeavor of Christian unity as a basis for a new evangelization in our time. As a Catholic bishop under obedience to the pope, I can only marvel at how the appeal of St. John Paul II is beginning to find a remarkable answer through his successor who hails from one the world's great intersections of Catholicism and Evangelicalism. Pope Francis is a witness to God's impatience with division within the Body of Christ. He is also an apostle of the joy that springs from the heart of the Good Shepherd, who continues to draw all people to himself.

Conclusion

Joseph Tosini

In the well-known Sermon on the Mount, Jesus begins by revealing what every human heart longs for: *supreme happiness*. Each verse begins with the word "blessed" (*beatitude*, which in Latin means "ultimate happiness"), then Jesus indicates the way to get there (see Matthew 5:3-11). In summing up the beatitudes I believe Jesus is saying that supreme happiness is a result of discovering the meaning of our existence, which is found in God alone. He reinforces the necessity of making this our first priority by juxtaposing it to what's basic for sustaining our physical life: food and shelter (see Matthew 6:31). He then proceeds to reveal what God wants from each of us so we will have that happiness: "Strive first for the kingdom of God" (Matthew 6:33).

In his Letter to the Romans, Paul gives a definition of the Kingdom. "For the kingdom of God is not food and drink but righteousness and peace and joy in the Holy Spirit" (Romans 14:17). I believe what he is saying is that, contrary to what we usually believe, our cultural identities are not the glue that bind us to the eternal reality for which we were created. Instead, righteousness, peace, and joy in the Holy Spirit are what bring us supreme happiness. At this point, the logical question that needs to be answered is, what does "righteousness and peace and joy in the Holy Spirit" mean and how do we get it?

If you have ever put a jigsaw puzzle together you know how important it is to have the picture of what it will look like when it's done. That answer is usually given on the cover of the puzzle box. There are very good reasons for this besides just the necessary positioning of the pieces. It also displays what the final product will look like. Why would we want to spend hours or days putting together something we might not want to see when it is completed?

When Jesus told us to "strive first for the kingdom of God," he gave us the picture of what that Kingdom would look like when it comes. Let's look at the picture the Lord gave us with his words and actions. When you address the Maker of heaven and earth—who is omnipotent, omnipresent, and omniscient—Jesus says, use the words "Our Father." So begins the picture of family. We are joined to him as family. The rest of the prayer he gives the apostles extends the relational theme among each member of that family. The Kingdom of God, then, has everything to do with relationship. Relationship with God: "Your kingdom come. Your will be done." Relationship with those around us: "Forgive us our debts as we also have forgiven our debtors." Put your relationship with God and your relationship with your brothers and sisters in the first place, and you will be letting God's will be done. And the Kingdom of God will come. In the end, the glory of the coming Kingdom is a unified family living on a restored earth. That is the meaning of Paul's definition in his Letter to the Romans: righteousness (right relationship), peace (the security that comes from being in right relationship), and joy (the eternal expression of God's Kingdom).

In the stories you have read in this book, the recurring theme is love resulting in unity. To drive home the point that the unity presented here is not uniformity, I will use an analogy from the card game poker. In playing poker there is a set value placed on each possible combination of cards received. If someone has a pair of 9s and someone else has a pair of 10s, the 9s yield to the 10s. It is not that the 9s have no value, but they need to submit to the greater value, the 10s. There are a number of different combinations of hands that can occur, yet all who play know when their hand needs to yield to the other. There is, however, one hand that rarely gets dealt, called the "royal flush." The royal flush is the supreme hand to which every other hand must yield. It is the hand that cannot lose. If you have this hand, you can gamble all you possess with confidence. You will win.

The Kingdom of God is God's royal flush. Jesus told us to pray for its appearance on earth as it is in heaven (see Matthew 6:9-13). In our preface we spoke of the significance of Jesus' prayer in the seventeenth chapter of John's Gospel. He asked that all who have experienced and continue to experience his grace and mercy, acknowledging him as their Lord and Savior, be brought together into the unity of the triune God (see John 17:20-21). Understanding this is not simply an intellectual pursuit. It is our calling as Christians. Jesus who lives in us through the Holy Spirit continues to proclaim and display his gospel through our unity. "God is making his appeal through us" (2 Corinthians 5:20). Jesus calls his apostles his friends and tells them that his Father is now their Father. Jesus implores us to be brothers and sisters of one another with one Father, to be a family. Only in this way will the world believe who he is. The Kingdom of God is Jesus, with the whole Trinity, living in us and among us through our constant and enduring love for one another. In his prayer in John chapter 17, Jesus plays the royal flush hand. To it all other hands or understandings must yield. All understanding of the Kingdom of God must start here and be seen through this lens.

The goal of sin is division. It never stops dividing until we are completely alone. The goal of salvation is unity. It never stops drawing us together by grace into the love and unity of God. This is our destiny; this is the eternal purpose of God; this is the mission of the Church. This will display to principalities and powers the love of God that surpasses knowledge (see Ephesians 3:10, 19).

At the close of our last meeting with Pope Francis I wanted to express our gratitude to him for meeting with us.

I mentioned a story from when I was a young boy and my grandfather would take me to the store for ice cream. He often would ask me this question before I could order our ice cream: "Joseph, do you want love?" I, of course, wanted an ice cream. He would repeat the question until I said, "Yes, Grandpa. I want love." He then gave me a word of wisdom that has stayed with me my whole life. In his broken English he would say, "If you want love, you need to give love." Then he would add, "God first gives us love, then we give it back." I mentioned this story as an example of how we felt being with Pope Francis. He gave us love and acceptance and we wanted to give it back to him. The reason we speak of pursuing love rather than unity is because unity is the gift of God that results from following Jesus' command to love (see John 13:34).

Our prayer for each of you is that you will be an initiator. Chiara Lubich, founder of the Focolare Movement, says, be "the first to love by always taking the initiative, without waiting for the other one to go first. This can be a real challenge for us, testing the authenticity and purity of our love."[10] She points out that in John's Gospel and Letters, God is always the first to love, so to love as God does puts us in the role of the initiator.

> "God's love was revealed among us in this way: God sent his only Son into the world so that we might live through him. In this is love, not that we loved God but that he loved us and sent his Son to be the atoning sacrifice for our sins. Beloved, since God loved us so much, we also ought to love one another" (1 John 4:9-11).

Jesus' new commandment, "love one another" (John 13:34), brings us into a new era. It is a radical call, as Augustine of Hippo writes: "This love renews us and makes us new persons, heirs of the New Testament who have a new song to

---

10. Lubich, *The Art of Loving*, p. 49.

sing."[11] The people who contributed to this book are not looking to be unifiers by convincing everyone to embrace their views or styles. They are, however, asking all of us to take seriously Jesus' prayer that we as his followers make his prayer our own. They are betting everything on Jesus' royal flush.

Our desire is that you have found hope in this small book. Hope that the Church Jesus said he would build through his life, death, and resurrection will become more visible and appealing. The human heart longs for the Kingdom Jesus proclaimed through his life. We as his followers have been called to continue to proclaim that Kingdom through our lives together. So, I say to you, the reader, join us in the hope-filled journey. Become initiators of friendship. Buy someone who isn't in your particular tribe of Christianity a cup of coffee or an ice cream. Hear their journey and pray that as followers of Jesus we might see each other not only through the eyes and hearts of siblings but through the eyes of the Father. *Father, help me to see, think, and feel for my brothers and sisters what you see, think, and feel for them.*

---

11. St. Augustine, Homilies on the Gospel of John, Hyde Park, NY: New City Press 2009.

Author Biographies

Joseph Tosini

Joseph sees himself as an ordinary man on a quest to make a difference. He used to question the meaning and reason for everything going on inside and around him. But once he was able to connect with his purpose in life, everything changed. As an ordained minister, Joseph's mission-oriented work around the world has honed his ability to build relationships and effect change. He leads through friendship, teaching and giving with a strong belief that any person, no matter how ordinary they feel, can choose to do extraordinary things. Joseph has authored several books about conflict resolution in families and organizations. His books include *She Called Me Dad* and *Is There Not A Cause?: Beyond the Disappointment of Aimless Christianity*. Joseph and his wife Mary have five children and four grandchildren.

Mike Herron

Mike is a minister, composer, and author who travels worldwide sharing the good news of Jesus Christ. An accomplished pianist, he ministers in worship, preaching and teaching with a special sensitivity to the Holy Spirit. He is a founding member of the John 17 Movement. He and his wife Marsha live in Houston, Texas. They are the parents of three married children and grandparents of eight.

Don Curry

Don is from northern New York, where he presently resides with Mary, his wife of thirty-seven years. After nine years as an engineer with General Motors, Don left to become the principal of a private Christian school associated with New

Testament Church (NTC) in Massena, New York. Don became the pastoral team leader of NTC in 1994 and continued planting and strengthening local churches in the United States, Europe, Canada, and Colombia. Presently Don and Mary are planting a church in Plattsburgh, New York, while Massena continues to be their base and home. They have four adult children.

Gary Kinnaman

Gary served as senior pastor of Word of Grace Church in Mesa, Arizona, for twenty-five years. Under his leadership, the church grew to an average weekend attendance of over 4,500. Gary has published a dozen books and he now serves as a pastor at large, mentoring and networking church, government, and marketplace leaders to serve the Phoenix area. Gary currently serves as the Phoenix ministry mobilizer for the American Bible Society. He is a graduate of Biola University, Arizona State University, Fuller Theological Seminary, and Western Conservative Baptist Seminary. He and his wife Marilyn have three children and nine grandchildren.

Bishop Eduardo Nevares

The Most Reverend Eduardo Alanis Nevares grew up in a loving, devout Roman Catholic family. His parents were not rich, but they sent all of their children to Catholic school. After the four older children went to school, Eduardo and his mother would attend daily Mass. Seeing his mother's love and devotion for the Eucharist began to instill in him a desire to be a priest. He began his priesthood as a Missionary of Our Lady of La Salette in 1981. He also served as the pastor of St. Patrick Parish in Lufkin, Texas, and was later incardinated into the Diocese of Tyler, Texas, in May 2007. He served as vice rector of the Pontifical College Josephinum in Columbus, Ohio, after serving as the co-director of vocations in the Diocese of Tyler from 2002 until 2008. Bishop Nevares was ordained as the first Auxiliary Bishop for the Diocese of Phoenix in 2010 at St. Thomas Aquinas

Parish in Avondale. He continues to "Serve the Lord with Gladness," as his episcopal motto says, to the present day.

Bishop Thomas Olmsted

The Most Reverend Thomas J. Olmsted is the fourth Bishop of the Diocese of Phoenix. Prior to his arrival in Phoenix he served as Bishop of Wichita, after having served as the rector/president of the Pontifical College Josephinum, a Catholic seminary in Columbus, Ohio. For sixteen years, Bishop Olmsted lived in Rome, Italy, where he obtained a master's degree in theology and a doctorate in canon law, and worked more than nine years in the Secretariat of State of the Holy See. During his years serving in the Holy See, he resided at the Pontifical North American College and assisted seminarians with spiritual direction.

Sharon & Peter Poppleton

Peter and Sharon have been married for forty years. They have three sons and ten grandchildren. With his theology background, Peter has worked in various aspects of religious education publishing—training, sales, marketing, and product development—for over thirty years. Currently he serves as overall coordinator of City of the Lord, a Catholic Charismatic Community. He and Sharon have been with City of the Lord for forty years. Sharon was a stay-at-home mom and then worked as an English teacher, primarily with adult immigrants. Both Sharon and Peter have been active in the John 17 Movement from the beginning.

Joshua Ryan Butler

Joshua is a pastor at Imago Dei Community (Portland, Oregon) and author of *The Skeletons in God* and *The Pursuing God*. He has developed Imago Dei's city ministries in many areas, including foster care, human trafficking, and homelessness; and crafted international partnerships in areas such as clean water, HIV support, and church planting. Joshua enjoys writing worship music, striving to infuse theological depth and poetic imagination into the life of the local church. Joshua and his amazing wife Holly and their three awesome children enjoy spending time with friends over great meals and exploring their beautiful little patch of the world in the Pacific Northwest.

Linda Morris

Linda was born in Philadelphia, Pennsylvania. She attended Bellevue School of Nursing, Franklin School of Science and Arts, and Georgia State University. Linda is married to Burnett, a retired fire mechanic. They have four adult children and three grandchildren. Linda lived and worked in Saudi Arabia from 1995 to 1997. She began her relationship with Harvest Foundation in May 2001 as executive assistant to Bob Moffitt, founder and executive director. Linda currently serves with Harvest as associate staff, U.S. Field. She is a Harvest country coordinator and previously served as U.S. coordinator for Kenya and support for the Africa Working Group. At her church, Linda serves as outreach director and director of the First Pentecostal Church Community Center. She teaches a Samaritan Strategy class for adults and teaches evangelism and outreach for the church's discipleship classes and other groups.

Cal & Lisa Jernigan

Since 1987, Cal and Lisa Jernigan have served at Central Christian Church in Arizona, where Cal is the lead pastor. Central is a multisite church that averages an attendance of 10,000 people each weekend. They are both deeply engaged locally, nationally, and globally with an emphasis in the work of reconciliation and peacemaking. Cal and Lisa, along with their church, are intensely focused on the regions of Northeast Africa and the Middle East. Both travel extensively, speaking and leading others on this unique journey. Lisa is the co-founder of a global movement called Amplify

Peace, which launches women peacemakers through transformational encounters. They have two adult children and seven grandchildren.

Bishop Peter Smith

The Most Reverend Peter Smith was born and raised in South Africa, the oldest of six children in a strong Catholic family. After high school he served in the military. He obtained degrees in business and law and then joined a lay charismatic covenant community in the United States. Bishop Smith lived in Indiana and Minnesota before moving to Portland in 1996 to enter Mount Angel Seminary. He was ordained a priest for the Archdiocese of Portland in June 2001. He served in two parishes before studying canon law at The Catholic University of America in Washington, D.C. Thereafter he served as pastor of St. Rose Parish in Portland for seven years. In July 2013 he was appointed Vicar General and Moderator of the Curia for the Archdiocese of Portland. In March 2014, Pope Francis appointed him Auxiliary Bishop. He currently serves on the Ecumenism, Marriage and Family Life, and Canonical Affairs committees of the U.S. bishops' conference and is active in several ecumenical projects and ministries.

Peter Petrov

Peter is a Christian baptized as Orthodox, but brought up in a Protestant community. He comes from Bulgaria, a currently post-communist Eastern European country, and has witnessed the dramatic shift of lifestyle and religious and political points of view of a whole nation. As a movie director and apologist, he works on connecting the dots between science and religion through the art of cinema. Since he has been passionate about Christian unity since his childhood, this is the most significant theme that inspires him in life and art.

Brian and Gina Kruckenberg

Brian and Gina, residents of Phoenix, Arizona, have been married for eighteen years and have three children. Brian holds B.A., M.S., J.D., and D.Min. degrees and worked in corporate law before his transition to full-time ministry in 2004. Gina earned a B.A. in Fine Arts and worked as a human resources recruiter before taking on the more challenging role of stay-at-home mom in 2001. Brian and Gina started New City Church in downtown Phoenix with friends in 2010, where Brian serves as lead pastor and Gina serves in women's ministry and event coordination. New City reaches thousands of young people in the city's rapidly growing urban core. They also launched the art gallery New City Studio as a part of the church's ministry. Brian often speaks at conferences in the areas of faith and work, church leadership, and church planting. He sits on the board of the Orchard Group, an organization that starts churches in what are considered "hard to reach" cities, like New York City, San Francisco, Cape Town, and Paris.

Patrick Markey

Patrick Markey is the executive director of the Diocesan Fiscal Management Conference, an association of Catholic diocesan finance officers in the United States and Canada. He worked for many years prior to that running grant programs at the United States Conference of Catholic Bishops and in religious publishing. He is a long-time member of the Focolare Movement and has served many Catholic organizations, including six years as a regional director of the Focolare Movement and on the executive committee of Religions for Peace USA. His volunteer work has largely focused on leadership development, especially youth and young adult faith formation.

Michael Rudzena

Michael Rudzena is the founder of Trinity Grace Church in the Tribeca neighborhood of Manhattan, where he lives with

161

his wife Kyndi and their three children. He helps lead the Center for City Renewal in NYC, focused on issues of justice, civility, and vocation. Michael writes and speaks as a sacred activist, connecting the practices of silence, stillness, and solitude to the demands of our conflicted world.

Ryan Nunez
As a third generation pastor, Ryan took a fun detour in his college years by studying to be a scientist. After many years of school and finishing his doctoral degree he felt called to full time ministry. Ryan has been the lead pastor at Palm Valley Church, with multiple campuses in Phoenix, Arizona, since 2014. Ryan and his wife Adrienne are passionate about reaching people far from God. They started Palm Valley Church with three other couples under the leadership of the founding pastor, Greg Rohlinger, and his wife Lori, back in 2000. Ryan's incredible family, Adrienne and their four kids, keep him on his toes and full of fun and crazy stories!

Ken Costa
Ken is a businessman, philanthropist, author, and public speaker. He served as vice-chairman of UBS Investment Bank, where he worked for over thirty years, before being named chairman of Lazard International. Ken is also chairman of Worship Central and dean of the Leadership College London. He is chairman of the Archbishop of Canterbury's Reconciling Leaders Network, a charity aimed at providing reconciliation training for leaders. Ken has written three books: *God at Work, Know Your Why: Finding and Fulfilling Your Calling in Life*, and *Strange Kingdom*. He is emeritus professor of commerce at Gresham College. Ken is married to Dr. Fiona Costa and they have four children.

Mark Buckley
Mark is the founder of Living Streams Church in Phoenix, Arizona. He has been involved in planting churches and

establishing ministries for over forty-eight years. Mark has been married to Kristina since 1973. They have four children and four grandchildren. Mark is currently the president of Grace Association, a network of church and ministry leaders in Arizona. He also leads Mark Buckley Ministries LLC, which focuses on strengthening and encouraging local pastors, leaders, and churches. Mark often speaks in churches and conferences, writes Reflections newsletters and has been a frequent radio guest and host.

Matt Maher

Since his 2008 major label debut, Matt Maher has become a staple in the artistic and songwriting community. A nine-time GRAMMY nominee, he has garnered multiple radio successes writing and recording songs like "What A Friend," "Lord, I Need You," "Hold Us Together," "Christ Is Risen," "Because He Lives (Amen)," and "Your Grace Is Enough." Matt has penned songs recorded by Chris Tomlin, Crowder, Third Day, Matt Redman, Hillsong, Casting Crowns, Jesus Culture, and Bethel, among others. Matt has written or co-written seven No. 1 radio singles. He performed in Rio de Janeiro in front of Pope Francis and a crowd of 3 million people at World Youth Day, and performed in Philadelphia as part of the World Meeting of Families with The Fray, Aretha Franklin, Juanes, and Jim Gaffigan, among others. Matt was recently also awarded his first RIAA Gold certification for his popular single "Lord, I Need You."

Bishop James Massa

The Most Reverend James Massa is an Auxiliary Bishop of the Roman Catholic Diocese of Brooklyn. A graduate of Boston College and Yale University's School of Divinity, Bishop Massa pursued his doctorate in systematic theology at Fordham University in New York. He wrote his dissertation under the late Cardinal Avery Dulles. While serving in various pastoral roles, and later on the faculty of several seminaries, Bishop Massa has lectured and published on topics pertaining to ecumenism and the theology of the Church. In 2005, Bishop Massa was named the executive director of the United States Conference of Catholic Bishops' Secretariat for Ecumenical and Interreligious Dialogue, where he coordinated national meetings between Catholic leaders and their dialogue partners from other faith traditions. Three years later, Pope Benedict XVI appointed him a consultor to the Pontifical Council for Interreligious Dialogue and a member of the Joint Working Group between the Holy See and the World Council of Churches. Since 2013 he has served in the Brooklyn Diocese as the Moderator of the Curia and Vicar for Catholic Education. In 2015 Pope Francis named him an Auxiliary Bishop with the Titular See of Bardstown, Kentucky.

Letter to Giovanni Traettino

Dear brother,

You have kindly informed me that from 20 to 22 February next a Meeting of Reconciliation will be held in Phoenix between Evangelicals and Catholics, in which you will take part. This news gave me great joy and made me more conscious of the need for reconciliation in this week in which we pray for Christian unity.

I hope that this meeting will draw down the Lord's blessings so that we can persevere along the path to unity. We who have received the one baptism long for full communion; this is a grace of the Lord which we must fervently implore. In some parts of the world Christians are being attacked and rejected, at times violently. Those who attack us do not distinguish between Orthodox, Lutherans, Evangelicals or Catholics; they know only that these brethren are Christians. As far as they are concerned, we are all the same. And in these attacks many of our brothers and sisters have given their lives in witness to Jesus Christ. In such places they are experiencing the ecumenism of bloodshed, the ecumenism of martyrdom. This should impel us all the more to seek paths of unity in our daily lives.

Dear brother, I will accompany you with my prayers in these days of the Meeting, asking God's blessings upon all taking part. By praying for one another, we exercise that spiritual ecumenism which accompanies all our actions. I ask you and all those taking part in the Meeting kindly to pray for me as well.

May the Lord bless all of you.

From the Vatican, 22 January 2014

Fraternally,

Franciscus

Video Message from Pope Francis to a John 17 Gathering in Phoenix, Arizona on May 23, 2015

Sisters and brothers, may the peace of Christ be with you.

Forgive me for speaking in Spanish, but my English is not good enough for me to express myself properly. I speak in Spanish but, above all, I speak the language of the heart. I have the invitation you sent me for this celebration of Christian unity, this day of reconciliation. And I wish to join you from here. "Father, may we be one so that... the world may believe you sent me" (Jn. 17:21). This is the slogan, the theme of the meeting: Christ's prayer to the Father for the grace of unity. Today, Saturday May 23, from 9:00 in the morning until 5:00 in the afternoon, I will be with you spiritually and with all my heart. We will search together, we will pray together for the grace of unity. The unity that is budding among us is that unity that begins under the seal of the one Baptism we have all received. It is the unity we are seeking along a common path. It is the spiritual unity of prayer for one another. It is the unity of our common labor on behalf of our brothers and sisters, and all those who believe in the sovereignty of Christ.

Dear brothers and sisters, division is a wound in the body of the Church of Christ. And we do not want this wound to remain open. Division is the work of the Father of Lies, the Father of Discord, who does everything possible to keep us divided.

Together today, I here in Rome and you over there, we will ask our Father to send the Spirit of Jesus, the Holy Spirit, and to give us the grace to be one, "so that the world may believe" (Jn. 17:21). I feel like saying something that may sound controversial, or even heretical, perhaps. But there is someone who knows that, despite our differences, we are one. It is he who is persecuting us. It is he who is persecuting Christians today, he who is anointing us with the blood of martyrdom. He knows that Christians are disciples of Christ: that they are one, that they are brothers and sisters! He doesn't care if they are Evangelicals, or Orthodox, Lutherans, Catholics or Apostolic... he doesn't care! They are Christians. And that blood of martyrdom unites. Today, dear brothers and sisters, we are living an ecumenism of blood. This must encourage us to do what we are doing today: to pray, to dialogue together, to shorten the distance between us, to strengthen our bonds of brotherhood.

I am convinced it will not be theologians who bring about unity among us. Theologians help us, the science of the theologians will assist us, but if we hope that theologians will agree with one another, we will reach unity the day after Judgement Day. The Holy Spirit brings about unity. Theologians are helpful, but most helpful is the goodwill of us all who are on this journey with our hearts open to the Holy Spirit!

In all humility, I join you as just another participant on this day of prayer, friendship, closeness and reflection. In the certainty that we have one Lord: Jesus is the Lord. In the certainty that this Lord is alive: Jesus is alive, the Lord lives in each one of us. In the certainty that he has sent the Spirit he promised us so that this harmony among all his disciples might be realized.

Dear brothers and sisters, I greet you warmly, with an embrace. I pray for you. I pray with you. And I ask you, please, to pray for me. Because I need your prayers in order to be faithful to what the Lord wants from my Ministry.

God bless you. May God bless us all. Thank you.

Letter to John 17 Meeting to be held in New York

From the Vatican, 17 November 2015

Dear Brothers and Sisters in Christ,

You have kindly informed me that on 6 December next a Meeting of Reconciliation between Evangelicals, Pentecostals and Catholics will be held in New York. This news, coming shortly after my visit to your city, fills me with joy because it promotes and encourages the cherished journey, from which there is no turning back, toward full Christian unity. This has always been "God's dream". This is the prayer of our Lord Jesus Christ!

My own prayer is that the Lord of the Church may pour out his Spirit upon your Meeting and give new life and impetus to your desire for fellowship and your relationships. May he renew you in our shared calling to be ambassadors and ministers of reconciliation. Let us together intercede for a "new day" in relationships between Evangelicals, Pentecostals and Catholics of your great metropolis, a point of encounter and a strategic crossroads of languages, cultures and nationalities.

I pray too that your initiative, in fraternal and respectful union with others already in course throughout your country, may advance the reconciliation between Christian denominations which we desire and need, and may thus become a sign of renewal and of hope for the entire Church.

Today, I here in Rome and you in New York, will ask our heavenly Father to enlighten us with a renewed revelation of the grace which unites us in Christ. In him we are rooted; he is our one foundation. He is the Lord! To him we have been converted to him we have entrusted our lives. We confess him and we adore him! We have been born of the same seed! We are brothers and sisters. To him be glory in our lives and in the Church for all ages, world without end. Amen.

Message to the Meeting of Reconciliation between Evangelicals, Pentecostals and Catholics, New York, December 6, 2015

Dear brothers and sisters, on this day of praise and worship, friendship and reflection, I am united with you. In all humility I join you as one of the participants in the Meeting. In the certainty that we have one Lord, for Jesus is the Lord, and he lives in each of us! In the certainty that the Holy Spirit is the torrent of which each of us has been given to drink! I bless you and ask your blessing. And I cordially embrace you. Receive my loving embrace. And I ask all of you who take part in the Meeting, please, to remember to pray for me as well!

May the Lord bless you.

Fraternally,

Franciscus

Notes

Notes

Notes

New City Press

New City Press is one of more than 20 publishing houses sponsored by the Focolare, a movement founded by Chiara Lubich to help bring about the realization of Jesus' prayer: "That all may be one" (John 17:21). In view of that goal, New City Press publishes books and resources that enrich the lives of people and help all to strive toward the unity of the entire human family. We are a member of the Association of Catholic Publishers.

www.newcitypress.com
202 Comforter Blvd.
Hyde Park, New York

Periodicals
Living City Magazine
www.livingcitymagazine.com

 Scan to join our mailing list for discounts and promotions or go to www.newcitypress.com and click on "join our email list."